I0569231

Girl, JUMP!

Girl, JUMP!

BUILDING YOUR FINANCIAL SAFETY NET TO LEAVE AN ABUSIVE RELATIONSHIP AND RECLAIM YOUR FREEDOM

Justine De Peralta

FREE WORKBOOK!

As a way of saying thanks for your purchase, I'm offering a FREE workbook that's exclusive to readers of

Girl, JUMP!: Building Your Financial Safety Net to Leave an Abusive Relationship and Reclaim Your Freedom

Research shows that taking notes significantly improves fact recall. That's why I created this workbook–to give you the extra boost you need to take action quickly and start living a fulfilling life today.

Go to
www.justinedeperalta.com/girljump

or

scan the QR code below

to download your FREE workbook today!

TO MY PARENTS,

Thank you for your unconditional love and support. I've learned from both of you that it is possible to be strong *and* kind. I love you.

**TO THE STRONG, PATIENT, AND
KIND WOMEN IN MY LIFE,**

When I was broken, you picked my pieces up and gently handed them to me. You created space for me and watched me put myself back together. The truth is that I wouldn't have been able to heal without your love, patience, and friendship. I am forever grateful.

TO MARK,

You've created a space for me to thrive as my authentic self. Thank you for loving all of me. I love you.

TO MY FORMER SELF,

Thank you for not giving up and for finding ways to continuously love yourself in darkness and in light.

Disclaimer

This book contains material of a highly sensitive nature including domestic violence, abuse, assault, and strong abusive language that may be triggering or upsetting for some individuals. While the author has taken great lengths to ensure the subject matter is handled in a compassionate and respectful manner, it may be troubling for some readers. Please engage in self-care as you read this book.

If you or someone you know is in immediate danger, please contact your local police. If you or someone you know is experiencing abuse, please contact your local police and the National Domestic Violence Hotline for help at (800) 799-7233.

All the events in this book are true to the best of the author's memory. Some names, places, and identifying features have been changed to protect the identity of certain parties. The views expressed in this book are solely those of the author.

Additionally, the information provided in this book is for educational purposes only. It is not intended to be a source of financial or legal advice. Financial strategy and planning should be done only after consulting with a professional.

Contents

Introduction

In January 2013, I packed my bags and embarked on a journey halfway across the world to Istanbul, Turkey. I had accepted a position teaching at a private school. Traveling and immersing myself in different cultures had always been a passion of mine, and I was eager to take on this new challenge.

I arrived in Istanbul on a chilly, rainy night. After going through Customs, I spotted a man holding a sign with the name of the school written on it, along with my own name. As I walked towards him, I smiled then greeted him. In somewhat broken English, he welcomed me to the city and offered to take me to my apartment. During the car ride, I gazed out the window at the bright lights and buildings. I had started studying Turkish a few months back, but it seemed as though everything I learned flew out the window as I attempted to read the names of streets, signs, and buildings.

It took forty-five minutes before we pulled up to a dimly lit street and came to a stop. The neighborhood was cold and dark as I made my way down the cobbled pathway. Nevertheless, I was filled with enthusiasm, excitement, and anticipation. I would be staying in a women-only apartment with fellow teachers from the school.

Upon arrival, I had the chance to meet one of my two roommates. She was from South Africa and had been teaching at the school for a couple of years. She gave me a quick tour of the apartment before kindly excusing herself to her room for the night. I unpacked my belongings, showered, and gently eased myself into bed. By the time my head hit the pillow, I was asleep.

The next morning, my roommate and I were drinking coffee when the front door of our apartment opened. A woman with bright blue eyes and blonde hair entered. She smiled and introduced herself.

"Hi, I'm Kali."

I waved in response. "Hi, I'm Justine! Want to join us for coffee?" Kali put her luggage in her room, then joined us in the kitchen.

"Where are you from?" I asked.

"South Africa," Kali replied.

Our other roommate exclaimed, "Me too!"

We spent the rest of the morning getting to know each other better. Kali and I clicked immediately. My instincts told me that she and I were destined to be great friends.

One evening, Kali and I returned home from work and went to the kitchen to prepare dinner. I noticed Kali looking down at her pack of cigarettes.

"What's wrong?" I asked.

"They're smoking my cigarettes!" She shook the box at me.

"Who is?" I frowned.

"The owners!"

To our shock, it became apparent that the owners of the building were entering our apartment while we were at work without our consent. Although we were unsure about whether it was them who were smoking the cigarettes, they were the only ones that we knew of who had access to our apartment. Putting this assumption aside, we did know that someone was smoking in our apartment because Kali would throw away her cigarette butts in the morning before we left for work and our other roommate did not smoke. When we would return, there would be new cigarette butts in the ashtray.

A few days after this unsettling incident, the owners began accusing us of allegedly violating the rules by bringing men into our apartment. I asked them to show me proof of their accusations, but they were unable to. These accusations were baseless, but it marked the first time in my life someone had aggressively accused me of something I had not done. I knew I had to find a new, safer place to live.

Little did I know this incident would serve as foreshadowing of the tumultuous year ahead.

Despite my positive, go-getter attitude, I quickly realized that life in Istanbul was going to be much more difficult than I anticipated. I worked seven days a week, 10-hour shifts, for very little pay. I lived paycheck-to-paycheck, and would often have to choose between buying food and paying rent. When I asked my boss for extra work, he offered me an evening position teaching Business English to a private company twice a week. The office was only a few blocks down from the school and my apartment, so I decided to take it. This was the best financial decision I made that year. Not only did extra money help with my living expenses, but it also helped bring just a little more peace to my already chaotic life.

With that being said, making more money didn't make me better at managing my money. The last thing I wanted to think about was budgeting and saving money when I was quite literally fighting for my life. Being in survival mode fostered an environment of unhealthy decisions around my relationships, health, and finances. I convinced myself that spending my money on alcohol, cigarettes, and partying would get rid of my problems.

Unfortunately, my problems didn't go away.

They got worse.

Outside of work, the male landlord wanted to move into our female-only apartment without our consent, forcing me to find somewhere else to live...again. I moved a total of four times during my time in Istanbul. Above all, there was civil and political unrest unfolding from the Gezi Protests; an environmentalist push-back at Gezi Park.

I was mentally, emotionally, and physically exhausted. Being in survival mode demands a certain level of vigilance. This is a skill one acquires through struggle and adversity. If you're reading this book, you might already be familiar with the concept. However, like many things in life, this state of awareness is not linear. There will be moments when your awareness can slip away in the blink of an eye.

The first time I was physically assaulted was on my walk home from work. At the time, I lived in an apartment at the bottom of a small hill less than half a mile from the school. I worked off one of the busiest streets in Istanbul, so there was usually someone around even late at night. My walk started off in a busy, well-lit area, filled with shops and restaurants. As I continued past the shops and restaurants, the noise disappeared into the background. The only thing I could hear were my footsteps hitting the cobblestone beneath me.

Once I reached the front door of my apartment building, I began to put my keys into the lock when someone came up behind me. Startled, I quickly turned around to find a man forcefully pushing me against the door. In a state of panic, I screamed. I punched his chest and managed to push him off to the side. As I tried to maneuver around him, he aggressively grabbed my arm. I turned around and began to hit his arm while I attempted to pull mine away.

Eventually, he let go of me and I bolted up the street screaming "Help! Help! Help, someone please!"

Despite my efforts, the onlookers simply walked in the opposite direction. I ran towards the main street and into a shop, where I frantically asked the cashier if he could see the assailant. When the coast was clear, I thanked the older man and quickly ran back to my apartment building. As I entered my apartment, my roommates greeted me, but I brushed past them and went straight to my room. Frustrated, overwhelmed, and scared, I cried myself to sleep that night. I didn't tell them what happened.

The morning after, I made the decision to have my guard up at all times. I refused to have something like that happen to me ever again. I became hyper vigilant...and angry. For the remainder of my time in Istanbul, I convinced myself that my anger and hypervigilance was a sign of strength; a belief which I would carry with me for years.

I left Istanbul in December 2013, and often told people that living there was one of the hardest years of my life. I experienced adversity in a way that I had not before. My experience there made me reflect on my strength and tenacity as well as my relationship with money. Living paycheck to paycheck was taxing on my mental and physical health. When I left, I promised myself that I would never go back to living paycheck-to-paycheck. But life has a funny way of teaching us lessons and testing our resilience.

Now I want to tell you another story. One that is just as important and significant.

Just over a year later, I would find myself in an abusive marriage that tested my mental, physical, and emotional health along with my finances. This is *that story*.

As a woman, you hear horror stories of domestic violence and abuse. According to the Centers of Disease Control and Prevention (CDC), "nearly twenty people per minute are physically abused by an intimate partner in the United States." Additionally, 95 percent of domestic violence victims are women. One in three women have been victims of some form of physical violence by an intimate partner within their lifetime. According to the American Psychological Association, victims of intimate partner violence lose a total of eight million days of paid work each year. Between 21-60 percent of victims lose their jobs due to the abuse. Still, even knowing this, we somehow convince ourselves that it would never happen to us. The harsh reality is that domestic violence and intimate partner violence can happen to anyone. It is not limited by factors such as race, age, social, or economical status.

For nearly a decade, I've wanted to share my story, but experienced an immense amount of shame, guilt, and fear that I needed to work through. Fear created barriers, preventing me from making meaningful decisions and living an authentic life. The biggest obstacle preventing us from living an intentional, present life is *fear.*

Fear of loss.
Fear of failure.
Fear of change.
Fear of judgment.
Fear of the unknown.

In order for us to confront our fears, we will focus on the importance of intention. By being intentional, you will be able to replace fear with purpose, mindfulness, and empowerment.

My journey of self-discovery and healing did not truly begin until I filed for divorce. Prior to that, I was in survival mode. For a *long time.* This healing process gave me a deep sense of desire and urgency to share my story and the lessons I learned. However, my intention is not to evoke sympathy from you.

In this book, I recount a part of my life filled with struggle, pain, and abuse. Rather than dwelling on what happened to me, I have made the intentional decision to give voice to my shame, guilt, and fear by sharing my story of tenacity, strength, and empowerment. I want to talk about how I turned my trauma into power; finding meaning, purpose, and strength through all of it. By finding myself, I no longer live as a prisoner of my past, but as a warrior of wealth.

According to Merriam-Webster, *wealth* is defined as an "abundance of valuable material possessions." While many people may primarily associate wealth this way, I believe

> wealth is defined by three concepts— health, finances, and time. All three are beautifully connected, creating a strong foundation for a self-loving authentic life.

True transformation takes place when you go from a place of *need* to a place of *want*.

I wrote this book to help women and domestic abuse survivors and victims go from a place of ***I need to get out*** to ***I want to reconnect and reclaim my relationship with money and myself.***

Do *you* want to:

- get out of a toxic relationship?
- identify your values and priorities?
- transform your unhealthy relationship with money?
- take control of your finances?
- construct and implement a financial plan based on your values?
- create an emergency fund and start putting money into it?
- pay down and eliminate bad debt?
- improve your credit score?
- live life on your own terms?

Last question: Are you willing to show up for yourself and do the work?

If you answered *yes* to one or more of these questions, then this book is for you.

Throughout this book, you will learn to:

- Identify emotional and financial abuse
- Develop a healthy money mindset
- Identify your *Why*
- Create an intentional budget
- Set up and fund an emergency fund
- Create and implement a debt repayment plan
- Legally document abuse
- Seek free/low cost legal assistance
- Recover and heal your inner self

This book is broken into three phases:

- **Phase 1: The Fog**
  First, we will delve into the early days of my relationship and the financial mistakes I made. The narrative here revolves around the hazy decision-making process influenced by emotions, excitement, and manipulation. I will highlight red flags that were present, but ignored in the midst of infatuation, denial, and fear; and set the stage for the challenges and lessons to come. At the end of each mistake, I identify the lessons learned, followed by next steps to move forward.

- **Phase 2: The Darkness**
  This is the darkest part of my journey, characterized by the realization of an abusive relationship and

the need to break free. Despite being a challenging time, this is also when I began the process of reclaiming my financial situation and life. Here, we are going to focus on the exact steps I took to create a financial safety net, including: transforming your money mindset, creating a sustainable budget, creating and funding an emergency fund, creating and implementing a debt management plan, and seeking legal assistance. This phase is a reflection of the resilience and determination needed to escape darkness and move closer to financial independence.

- **Phase 3: The Light**
  In this final phase, we will shift the focus to the aftermath of leaving an abusive relationship, and the journey towards recovery, healing, and empowerment. Here, we focus on three key areas—health, wealth, and relationships—and the changes needed to optimize your mental health and wellbeing.

To gain the most benefits, I highly recommend each section be read sequentially. Remember—we are starting from the bottom, with a clean slate. Additionally, I recommend downloading the workbook to give you the extra boost you need to take action quickly. You can download the free workbook now at www.justinedeperalta.com/girljump.

As you navigate this book, you will learn that money is not the most precious currency; *time* is. Unlike money, of which you can earn more, or possessions, that you can repeatedly purchase, time is universally finite; the one resource that you cannot extend or save. Since time is not renewable, we never experience the time that passed twice. The more we put towards our endeavors, the more likely we'll see progress and fulfill our aspirations.

As you read each chapter, I want you to remember that time doesn't stop for perfection, for the right moment, or for you to make a decision. It flows regardlessly, and it's up to you to use it wisely.

As someone who is stuck, you have taken a giant step forward to reclaiming your money, life, and time just by picking up this book. I'm so proud of you for being courageous and curious. Don't wait to get started and take action. This only gives your problems time to worsen.

Before we dive in, I leave you with this: If you're grateful for your life, you have to be grateful for all of it—the *happiness* and the *suffering*.

Here's my story.

Phase 1

THE FOG

Financial Mistake #1

FALLING IN LOVE WITH ONLY POTENTIAL, NOT REALITY

There's something to be said about what society has taught us about falling in love: That it's wildly romantic falling in love with who a person *could be,* and what a person *could* give you. This concept has been often depicted, in movies and fairytales, as a noble act of seeing the best in someone and supporting them through their growth. The problem with this perspective, however, is that it makes it easy to overlook the importance of accepting people for who they are in the present moment. Perhaps who they are in the present moment is not who you want to be with. I, too, am guilty of solely falling for potential.

Six months after I moved back to California, I packed my bags once more. With a one-way ticket in hand, I headed to New York City to begin the next chapter of my life: a graduate student at a prestigious university. After my experiences in Istanbul, I thought New York City would be a walk in the park.

After all, "if you can survive in New York City, you can survive anywhere." New York City represented freedom, excitement, and peace. It had its own version of grit, charm, and character; and I loved it.

On my first day of student orientation, I met Angie. She was from Los Angeles, like me, had big brown eyes, a beautiful smile, and contagious laugh. We hit it off immediately. Towards the end of the day, the school administrators suggested all students stop by their respective Advisor's office to introduce themselves. Since Angie and I were in different departments, I told her I would meet her later for happy hour drinks.

Sitting outside of my Advisor's office was a young woman with long brown hair and a warm smile. I asked her where she was from and she happily responded, "Germany! I'm Jules by the way!"

We started chatting and when it was my turn to meet my Advisor, Jules said, "I'll wait for you!"

Later, Jules and I met up with Angie to grab drinks at a neighborhood bar, and spent the rest of the evening talking and laughing. As Angie got up to leave for the night, I looked at Jules.

"One more?" I asked with a smirk on my face.

"Oh my god, yes!" she exclaimed.

I knew I met someone special that day.

When I wasn't in school or spending time with friends, I juggled two part-time jobs. On weekday mornings, I worked as a site operations specialist for a middle school in Harlem. In the evenings, I was a teacher trainer/coordinator for an ESL program, typically finishing work around 8pm.

On my way home one night, I stopped at The Tavern, a neighborhood bar and restaurant. I only wanted one drink, but I ended up staying for several, and watching the Lakers basketball game. After some friendly banter with the workers and locals (I found out the main bartender had the same birthday as me), I left feeling happy and excited. The warm, welcoming ambience made me feel connected to the community; and I was eager to embrace this next chapter of life with confidence.

The Tavern became my go-to place for hanging out with friends, enjoying a meal, and unwinding after a long day. On a chilly November evening, my friends and I were sipping our drinks when two unfamiliar men walked in. After a quick glance, I had a feeling they weren't locals. Their demeanor spoke volumes—meticulously styled hair, fitted clothing. The taller one had on a baseball hat and big, black puffy jacket. His hunched posture made him seem shorter. The *actual* short guy wore glasses and an unbuttoned dress shirt. In fact, he was two buttons away from completely revealing his chest and stomach. *'It's fucking freezing. I mean, it's the end of November **and** snowing outside! Why the open shirt?!'*

These guys stuck out like sore thumbs.

"They're European aren't they, Jules?" I whispered.

"I don't know. Maybe?"

As my friends and I continued our conversation, the two men approached our table. The short one striking up a conversation with me.

"Feo." He extended his arm and introduced himself.

"Feh-oh?" I repeated back to him, struggling with the pronunciation. We shook hands. "I'm Justine."

I introduced myself to his friend, Daniel, and the five of us hung out for the remainder of the evening. As the night continued, I spent the majority of the evening talking with Feo. With his shoulders pulled back, his chest out; Feo had an air of confidence about him. He spoke passionately about becoming a famous businessman one day, even moving from Spain to pursue his dreams.

"I want to be known all over the world!" His eyes sparkled with determination. His big ambitions and gutsy behavior of moving to another country resonated with me. I found myself drawn to him. In a sea of uncertainty, his clarity of purpose stood out to me. It was refreshing to meet someone with tangible dreams and the courage to pursue them.

As our conversation unfolded, he mentioned that he had been in New York City for less than a month. I found that surprising. By the way he spoke, it seemed that he had been in the United States for years. I felt an instant connection with him, and our conversation flowed effortlessly. When it was time to part ways, we exchanged numbers and said goodbye.

"What do you think?" I asked Jules as we walked back to my apartment.

Jules paused, her brows furrowing as she considered her next words. "I'm...concerned," she began slowly, her voice trailing off slightly before she found her rhythm again. "I didn't like how close he got to you or how eager he was to share his plans to become a successful businessman, almost like he's trying too hard to impress us." She let out a sigh and took a breath. Her expression turned skeptical. "And what really bothered me was how happy he got when he heard you were from California. He was almost *too* happy. The way he was acting, it just didn't sit right with me. It was just all... strange."

I walked silently and took it all in. I really valued my friendship with Jules and I admired how honest she was with me. I didn't think she was jealous, but concerned as my friend.

"Hmm...thank you for sharing that with me. I thought he was a bit strange at first too, but I did like how ambitious he was..." my voice trailed off. "What a long night. You know what? Let's talk about this later. Thanks for coming out tonight, girl!" I hugged Jules goodnight. "See you tomorrow!"

As I got ready for bed, I received a text message from Feo.

"Buenas noches, bella. Dulces sueños."

"Goodnight, Feo. Sweet dreams," I replied smiling, then closed my eyes to sleep.

For the first three months of our relationship, Feo knew all the right things to say that would calm my wounded soul. After my time in Istanbul, I had developed a new toughness and resilience. Both were driven by fear and masked by anger. I thought being tough meant I also needed to be angry. I developed a very *'don't fuck with me'* attitude. It wasn't until many years later I learned that my anger stemmed from pain, lack of self-love, and confidence. By not acknowledging my anger, I did not truly understand what I needed from myself, let alone what I needed from a partner.

So when he promised we would build a life together, I believed it. When he promised he would take care of us, I believed it. And when he promised to help me pay off my student loan debt, I believed it.

At the time, I had been drowning in $75,000 of student loan debt. Since I was still in school, I was told that I shouldn't start paying the loans back until after I graduated, so I held off on paying. Years later I learned that I indeed could have started paying down my subsidized loans while in school because they were not accruing interest, and I would have saved myself a *ton* of money.

At the time though, *'I'll cross that bridge when I get there'* was the attitude I embraced. To hear him say he would be willing to help me with my student loan debt, left me overcome with relief. Deep down, I didn't think I could pay my loans off by myself. My scarcity mindset and money avoidance scripts I told myself revealed the lack of self-belief I had in myself and my financial situation.

At the time, I thought this was love.

This person wanted to build a life with me, and take care of me financially. Who wouldn't want someone to do this, right? A year later, I would come to find out that he had no intention of building a life with me or fulfilling any of the promises he made.

Within the first two months of our relationship, Feo brought up marriage. It caught me completely off guard. We had only been in the early stages of getting to know each other, so I found it odd that he was already talking about getting married.

"At some point," I responded. From then on, he would bring it up frequently and my answer would be the same. However, this response would soon change and the decision to get married would come much earlier than expected.

In the wee hours of a chilly February day, I received a distressing call from Feo.

"I'm in trouble," he said.

"What happened?" Confusion and anxiety washed through me. One thing experience has taught me: Nothing positive ever comes after such words.

"I got arrested and fined," he muttered. He spoke so softly, I could barely hear him.

"WHAT!?"

He went on to tell me that on his way to visit me after work, he was arrested and fined by a station officer for jumping the subway turnstile.

"Why did you jump the turnstile?" I asked in disbelief.

"I wanted to avoid waiting another half hour for the next train to come. It was cold and I was tired..." he replied.

At first, I was overwhelmed with anger. I couldn't wrap my head around his decision to jump the turnstile. My mind raced.

Why would you be so idiotic to jump the turnstile?
Why act so recklessly when you know that you are working illegally?

In minutes though, my anger turned into worry. Another round of cascading thoughts filled my mind:

What's going to happen to us?
What will happen to him?
Will he get deported?

When the station officers released Feo, he was asked to appear in court a month later for his arraignment charges—trespassing in the third degree and theft of services. His decision that night forever changed the trajectory of my life. Even though he didn't bring up marriage when he got arrested, the situation still caused a sense of urgency and panic in our situation. With a little over a month until his court appearance, I experienced a whirlwind of emotions. From anger to frustration, hopeful to afraid. I struggled to make sense of everything. Faced with the possibility of his deportation, the decision to get married came sooner than anticipated. At the time, I found myself on the fence about marriage for several reasons. I didn't have the heart to tell my family I was considering marriage, especially to someone overstaying his visa. It weighed heavily on my mind and heart.

We had only been seeing each for a couple months; I knew there was still much to learn about Feo and him to know about me. Prior to his arrest, I hadn't been in a rush to get married. I was focused on getting my master's and enjoying my life in New York.

Not only was I struggling to gain a clear understanding of my situation, Feo repeatedly asked me what *we* were going to do. Initially, he made optimistic comments about our future, "We can have a life together," "I will take care of you," and "We are a great couple."

He would compliment me often: telling me how sweet and smart I was. These comments were often paired with nice gestures, taking me out for dinner or buying me nice gifts. I must admit, I enjoyed the attention; It made me feel loved. I found myself falling *in love* with the *potential* of a promising life together.

You remember that phrase, don't you?

However, despite all of this, I kept putting my decision off. I needed more time to think everything through. The longer I put it off, the more his comments began to shift. They were no longer about *us*, but about *me*

"If *you* love me, you'll do it."

"Do *you* want to see me deported?"

These comments often dominated our conversations and left me feeling guilty. During one of our conversations, I built up the courage to tell Feo why I was hesitant about getting married: I felt shame and guilt hiding the marriage from my parents. When I asked for his opinion on the matter, he supported *NOT* telling my family. I was shocked; a part of me expected him to push back on keeping it secret, but he didn't, and thought it would be better to tell them once he had 'made it' as a successful businessman. Having never met them, I understood his desire to present his best self to my family; and I thought him being a successful businessman would lend him more credibility.

When I asked him if he was going to tell his family, his response was an indisputable, "yes." Although I hadn't met them in-person yet, I had connected with them through video calls and text messages. I felt an overwhelming sadness wash over me. He didn't have any issues telling his family about us getting married, but was against me telling my own.

Despite my instinct telling me that something wasn't right, the internal narrative I told myself had much more power over my actions. My lack of confidence and reluctance to stand up for myself created a fog around my decision making. By focusing on the needs of my partner instead of mine, I was unable to identify his subtle gaslighting tactics sprinkled into my life.

Gaslighting is a psychological strategy where a person manipulates another person by questioning the other's own sanity and reality. When we would argue, Feo made comments like "I was on my way to see you the night I got arrested. If I wasn't on my way to see you, I would have never gotten arrested."

While I felt uneasy with these comments, I had convinced myself I didn't want to lose him. I was so focused on being a "good, loyal" partner I completely forgot to be "*good*" and "*loyal*" to who mattered the most—me.

The looming decision to get married weighed on me for weeks. One of the only people I could confide in was Jules. It was all I could talk about, I probably sounded like a broken record, but she was always patient and understanding. Her willingness to listen didn't mean she was on board. In fact, she vehemently expressed her dislike of Feo, and her concerns about our relationship.

I finally made the challenging decision to move forward. A few days before our courthouse wedding, I was in Washington, D.C. for a conference with Jules. I hadn't told her yet about the wedding. As we sat across the street from the White House, I felt the weight of an impending confession pressing on my tongue.

Come on, Justine. Just do it. It's Jules. She'll understand.
Fuck, what if she hates me?
You made your mind up. Just tell her already!

As I nervously played with my hands, I slipped the words out.

"I'm getting married." I stopped talking and gazed at the ground.

I couldn't look Jules in the eye; finally I summoned the courage to sheepishly look up, seeing shock and disbelief written all over her face.

She kept repeating a stunned "Wow."

When she snapped out of her trance, she asked, "Are you sure you want to do this?" Her questions came rapid-fire.

"Are you going to tell your parents?"

"What will they say?"

"Are you not telling anyone?"

"What made you decide to go through with it?"

"Are you *sure* you want to do this?!"

I struggled to answer.

"I don't think you should do this. Justine, think about it. You don't have to do this."

More than anything, her reaction left me feeling annoyed, defensive, and sad. I expected some pushback, but not like *this*. Unsuccessful, she eventually conceded, but there was a palpable sense of unease lingering in the air.

With a hesitant and exhausted sigh, Jules finally suggested, "Well, let's go grab drinks, I guess."

Inside the first neighborhood bar we found, laughter and excitement filled the air, and I wasted no time reaching for solace in a shot of whiskey. I wanted to drown out the echoes of doubt that took over my mind. I wanted to enjoy myself, but I found myself detached and disconnected.

"So I guess this is your bachelorette party…" Jules asked, taking a sip of her drink.

"Sure, I guess it can be!" My voice carried a forced cheerfulness.

Honestly, I felt like shit. I wanted excitement from Jules, and got the opposite.

I locked eyes with the bartender and asked, "Can I have another shot of whiskey?"

On the morning of my wedding, it was gloomy and chilly. Jules and Angie came over to help me get ready. I put on the white dress I bought from Forever 21 earlier in the week and started on my makeup. I would glance at Jules; and she would smile back. However, taking my pictures, I could see sadness behind her smile. I could sense a sadness within me too, but kept convincing myself getting married was the right decision. I fell in love with the *potential* of this relationship, and held onto the belief that everything would *work out*. Some might call it foolish. I called it optimistic. I did one last check in the mirror, looked at my friends and said, "I'm ready."

We walked slowly through the cold to the train station. The ride to the courthouse felt like the longest I'd ever been on. I was at war in my head. For every negative thought, I countered with a positive one that would happen in this next chapter of life. The narrative I told myself was that I was in a relationship with someone who was hardworking and ambitious, someone eager to grow with me, support me, and take care of me. I refused to acknowledge the negatives.

For as loud and chaotic New York City is, as we walked towards the courthouse, everything got quiet. I heard only the footsteps of my heels on the concrete. At the bottom of the courthouse stairs were Feo and Daniel. Feo smiled. And I smiled back.

"You look beautiful." His hand reached out for mine, and, cold and sweaty, I took his as we walked up the stairs.

Looking around I saw white dresses and dark suits sprinkled throughout the hallway. One woman had on a lacy red dress, her partner's bow tie matching it. Seeing other people getting married at the courthouse brought a peculiar sense of relief. I wasn't alone. There were others, like me, starting the next chapter of their lives that day. I failed to realize that their stories were, likely, vastly different from mine. By focusing on these surface-level observations, I was neglecting my own needs and feelings.

The court official called our names and within five minutes, I was officially a married woman.

What I Learned

I had fallen in love with the *potential* of someone, but know now that potential isn't what's important. It's who they currently are and their actions that make space for a healthy, strong relationship.

Don't get me wrong, there is something wildly romantic about falling in love with someone's potential. But the truth of the matter is when we fall in love with *only* potential, we set ourselves up for disappointment when they don't follow through. This can lead to trying to change them; and when they don't, well, enter resentment. Yes, people can change, but *genuine* change must come from self-motivated effort. It is not your responsibility to change them. Nor can you, in most cases. To do our best to avoid resentment, we need to focus on the *present* and our *own* needs.

Next Steps

The following are questions to ask yourself to gain a better understanding of your current financial situation:

- Do I have an emergency fund set up in a savings account?
- Does my financial situation align with my priorities?
- What are my current sources of income?
- Do I have any financial goals?
- Do I owe anyone any money?
- Do I have a working budget?
- Do I have any bad debt?
- Am I financially stable?

Reflecting on these questions can provide valuable insights on your financial health and give you a good starting point for making informed decisions to fulfill your own unmet needs and achieve financial stability.

Once you've gained a better understanding of what your financial needs are, it's important to understand who your partner currently is. The following are questions to ask yourself:

- Do they believe in their potential?
- Do their actions match their words?
- How do they handle stress, conflicts, and disagreements?
- Are they willing to have tough conversations during struggles?
- Do they hold themselves accountable or redirect blame?

- How do they react when they are *denied* what they want?

As we discussed above, falling in love with *only* potential, and not accepting who someone currently is, can be a financial mistake. Constantly hoping your partner's potential comes to fruition can lead to stress and conflict. Having unrealized expectations can cause instability later due to unmet promises or plans. Additionally, you may find yourself overlooking your relationship's current reality. Red flags and bad habits, such as gaslighting, blaming, temper, and unbalanced partnerships shouldn't be ignored. Only by seeing the potential and not the reality will your financial well-being be negatively impacted.

Financial Mistake #2

AVOIDING MONEY CONVERSATIONS

It takes a lot more than love to make a marriage work. Like many new things in life, there is a beginning stage to relationships. During this time, you engage in deep conversations to learn the person's character, goals, aspirations, beliefs, and values. Exploring these aspects helps build the foundation for a balanced, honest, sustainable relationship.

Somewhere between *how many siblings do you have* and *what was it like growing up in your hometown*, the topic of money often gets lost. In fact, it is often intentionally avoided. Money can be considered a taboo topic, particularly in the early stages of dating. You may start to wonder—*when* should we talk about money? *How* should we talk about money? *Who* is responsible for what? These questions can swarm your mind to the point of confusion. In turn, your confusion leads to overwhelm. Overwhelm spirals into frustration. Frustration to avoidance.

I didn't talk to Feo about money before we got married because I didn't know *what* to talk to him about. I didn't know my financial needs nor did I know *how* to speak up for myself.

17

I just knew that I needed to provide for both of us. There were two reasons I avoided talking about finances with Feo:

1. **I Was Not Financially Literate**
    My knowledge of financial literacy was lackluster before I got married. The most I knew was limited to saving and paying the monthly minimum on credit cards. What I failed to realize was the depth needed to not only support myself, but also a marriage. Feo and I didn't talk about our financial situations before we got married, nor did we talk about our finances during the marriage. Truth is, talks about our money were minimal, only surfacing when Feo needed something from me: opening a bank account for him, putting a deposit down on the apartment, or buying groceries. Other times we talked about money before getting married was Feo telling me how much money he was going to make in the future. Not the present.

2. **I Was Ashamed To Ask For Help**
    During the immigration process, the individual who signs the Affidavit of Support becomes the sponsor of the immigrant. As Feo's sponsor, I was financially responsible for him. Barely understanding the minimum responsibilities, I willingly signed these legal forms. I agreed to having sufficient income to take care of Feo and myself. I took on this massive legal responsibility without fully understanding the heaviness of it all. I thought I was capable and strong enough to shoulder everything on my own. As a result, I neglected my needs to support Feo, in hopes he would support me once he started making money. In hindsight, this was very dangerous: I was giving up my financial autonomy.

I was so overwhelmed with taking care of Feo that I neglected my own financial needs, and was avoiding honest conversations not just with Feo but with myself. Consequently, I experienced more negative feelings about money than positive ones. When I thought about my personal finances, I felt angry, upset, concerned, confused, and uncomfortable. These emotions were a result of my unmet needs.

Frustrated, I leaned on my marriage to fulfill these unmet needs— honesty, understanding, and safety. When my needs were unmet in my marriage, I stressed, and made impaired decisions based on fear and insecurity. As a result, I was $10,000 in credit card debt and had medical debt in collections. I found myself bitter and resenting my circumstances.

As I tried to navigate my stress, I struggled to communicate my feelings and needs to Feo. Discussing money with him was difficult; He was short-tempered, believed it was my responsibility to handle our finances, and refused to work through problems together.

What I Learned

At the end of the day, being in a relationship doesn't mean sacrificing your independence to meet the needs of the other person. You can absolutely maintain financial autonomy, and have joint finances while being committed to someone else. Being financially independent can mean having your own bank account, managing your own expenses, and setting your own financial goals. When you prioritize your own financial health, you avoid becoming dependent on your partner to support you and have better control over your money.

There are really three people in a relationship—you, your partner, and *us*. Not only do you have your own autonomy, but so does your partner. As you build your individual lives, you will come together to build the *us*, and that includes having difficult money conversations.

Reflecting on my situation, avoiding money conversations was my way of avoiding conflict, of dealing with embarrassment and shame I had regarding money. My failure to prioritize my financial health clouded my true feelings.

Next Steps

I knew our marriage had hit a serious rough patch financially when Feo was unwilling to work through our problems together. It's okay if your partner doesn't have the same financial upbringing as you. What matters is how you both work things out, so that needs are met on both sides. Ask yourself these questions the next time you navigate a difficult money conversation:

- Do I know how to express my needs and feelings to the other person?
- Can we walk away from a disagreement with both our needs met?
- What are their attitudes on money and financial habits?
- Do I understand the other person's needs and feelings?
- What is the purpose of this conversation?
- What do I hope to achieve?
- Am I being judgmental?
- Am I being judged?

Addressing your feelings and needs around money requires open communication and empathy. Spend time trying to gain a better understanding of what your feelings and needs are. This can help you feel more confident discussing money with your partner. Being proactive with your partner about your finances not only brings you closer together, but it can prepare you for uncomfortable conversations down the line.

Financial Mistake #3

LACK OF COMMUNICATION AND MAKING ASSUMPTIONS

In the weeks following our wedding, I began to notice a shift in Feo's attitude and behavior. His mood often fluctuated. One minute he was happy and laughing, then he would be agitated and angry. Being around him felt like walking on eggshells. Simple questions, like *how was your day* or *what would you like for dinner* could provoke his irritation; by all means, don't ask for help with something. When I did build up the courage to ask, his responses were dismissive or sharp.

"Why do you ask so many questions?!" he'd retort. It reached a point where I didn't know what was going to set him off, and was afraid to ask him.

As a result, I chose to stay silent. It was the easiest way to keep the peace. By choosing to stay silent, I didn't create opportunities for us to talk through our issues as a team. Additionally, I was indirectly teaching Feo that it was okay to continue to treat me like this.

At the time, we weren't living together. I shared an apartment with two roommates, and he lived with Daniel and two others. We decided to stay in our respective living arrangements until both our leases were up in August. We would see each other a few times a week, and as my twenty-sixth birthday approached, I felt a bubbling excitement. Feo worked seven days a week, so I wasn't sure if he would be working on my birthday. When his request to take the day off was approved, I was ecstatic. I looked forward to celebrating my birthday with him and my friends.

When my birthday came around, we spent the evening at a bowling alley. As the night unfolded, I noticed Feo didn't make much of an effort in getting to know anyone. I was uncomfortable seeing him by himself, and found myself making sure he was having fun frequently, partly out of empathy, but a small part of me was also worried he'd get upset.

When it came time to settle the bill, everyone chipped in their share, but the bill came back short by one person. I asked everyone if they paid and everyone said yes. Maybe it was presumptuous of me to expect my partner to cover my expenses. Feeling uncomfortable, I embarrassedly told everyone that I didn't pay and began to reach for my purse. My friends were confused and taken aback.

"Wait, did he not pay for you?!" All eyes turned to Feo.

I shook my head and nervously replied, "No, but it's okay."

My friends' eyes grew wide and their jaws dropped. They were furious.

"We will cover you!" My friends took the bill from my hand and shot Feo with a disgusted look.

When they asked why he didn't pay, Feo casually responded, "Oh, I didn't know." I made an excuse for him, saying it was because of cultural differences. But deep down, I was embarrassed and ashamed. The seemingly innocent excuse "I didn't know" would later become a recurring phrase he used to gaslight me.

For the remainder of the evening, I tried to make the most out of my birthday, but internally grappled with my overwhelming feelings of embarrassment and shame. When we got home, I heard a tirade of negative comments about the entire evening from him. Not only did he speak badly about my friends, which I found incredibly ironic because he had barely spoken to any of them, but he was also livid that I embarrassed him with the bill situation. He believed he did nothing wrong and it was all my fault.

While I shouldn't have assumed he would pay for me, communication before and after the situation could have been better on both our parts.

What I Learned

Talking about money can be uncomfortable, but is a necessary aspect in a relationship. It's easy to avoid these conversations, but that brings assumptions. Assumptions can be a result of necessary but neglected conversations. On my birthday, I assumed Feo would pay for me.

With so many perspectives on gender roles and finances it is especially important to communicate. Feo and I did not explicitly talk about who was paying for what beforehand, so when the time came to split the bill, there was no clear agreement. Looking back, I recognize that establishing clear communication and setting financial expectations could have prevented misunderstandings.

Next Steps

You and your partner can establish clear communication and set financial expectations by setting time aside for regular money conversations. Here are some tips to help you prepare for these conversations:

- Schedule time to check-in with your partner and stick to it.
- Pick a calm, neutral location with no distractions.
- Prepare for the conversation by outlining your key points, including your feelings and needs.
- Use positive language to set a positive tone. Remember, you are a team working towards the same goals.
- Avoid blaming or "you" language and, instead, use "I" statements.
- Avoid "Can you..." statements when making a request and, instead use "would you be willing to..." When a person is willing, they are agreeable and not coerced.
- Avoid "Can I..." statements. These statements may come off as asking for unnecessary permission or approval. Asking for permission to do something disempowers you and what you bring to the discussion.
- If the conversation becomes tense, ask your partner if they would be willing to take a break and revisit the conversation when calm.

Having regular money conversations with your partner creates relationship stability and balance. By discussing budgeting, investing, housing, groceries, and other financial topics, you can avoid overlooking needs and misunderstandings about expectations. During these money conversations, you both have the opportunity to be transparent about your financial situations, and work together as a team to reach your financial goals.

As mentioned in the previous chapter, if your partner is not willing to talk to you about money, this is a red flag and an early sign of financial abuse. Financial abuse is a form of abuse that gives one partner control and power in the relationship, leaving the other partner trapped. The partner in control may intentionally manipulate, intimidate, and threaten the other person. Opening credit cards under your name without your consent, preventing you from working, and taking your earned money are all examples of financial abuse. Knowing your partner's financial history and habits can prevent financial abuse later.

Financial Mistake #4

TRUSTING WORDS, NOT ACTIONS

While I enjoyed my time in New York City, I did not want to take out another student loan for the second year. Managing and shouldering the finances of my marriage was stressful enough! Instead, I made the bold decision to complete my two-year Master's program in just one year. I doubled down on my course load so I could be done with everything by the end of August.

In the months leading up to August, I received an exciting offer—a full-time position as Site Operations Manager for a non-profit edtech company! This new position would require relocating across the country. I was excited about this news as it would bring me closer to my family and back to California. Without hesitation, I happily accepted the position.

Exciting things were happening in my professional life, but my relationship with Feo was rocky. I tiptoed around his flippant behavior and dealt with his arrogance on a regular basis. Despite the challenges, I chose to give him the benefit of the doubt. I believed moving across the country would offer a fresh start to our relationship.

In August 2015, we packed our bags and headed to the North Coast of California to start the next chapter of our lives. At the time, my new salary was $65,000—the most money I had ever earned *and* the first time I had a salaried job. I thought this was sufficient to support both Feo and me, but the reality was that we were barely getting by. Prior to relocating, we did not discuss what our financial situation would look like—budget, savings, debt, income, expenses, and expectations. We didn't talk about any of it.

How could we? I didn't know how much money he actually had and whether he had any savings. I didn't ask questions and he did not willingly tell me. The money he made from his job in New York City could only support himself and I was unaware of any savings he had. For the move, I took on the financial responsibility by paying the moving costs upfront since he did not have a job yet or money to contribute at the time. This included Airbnbs, hotels, flights, transportation, meals, groceries, and furniture.

I pulled from my personal savings, which wasn't a lot to begin with, to put a $2000 deposit down on our apartment. It completely depleted my savings. I was incredibly stressed, but I knew that I was financially responsible for us. I didn't tell Feo I was stressed, but it must have come through anyway, because one night Feo told me that he wanted to start working. Technically, he was not allowed to without a working permit, but he insisted. In Spain, Feo went to school for hairdressing. He said he could look for a job at a hair salon. I was scared and hesitant at first, but we eventually reached an agreement that he would research job openings and make the necessary phone calls.

That just started a new problem.

When I'd come home from work and ask about his progress, he would get angry and defensive. "How am I supposed to look for work if I don't have a car?" he'd argue.

I reminded him of our agreement, emphasizing the agreed-upon-task, that he would research and *call* the businesses looking to hire.

"Did you try calling to see if the studios were hiring?" I asked.

"No," he snarled. "You should be grateful that I even *want* to work. Some guys wouldn't do anything and just let you work."

Frustrated, I quickly gave up on having this discussion with him. When the weekend approached, I drove Feo around looking for businesses that were hiring. Eventually, I spotted a barbershop and pulled over.

"It doesn't look like they're hiring..." Feo said.

"You never know. Just go in and ask," I responded.

Feo reluctantly got out of the car and entered the barbershop. Ten minutes later, he came out and walked towards the car.

"So? Any luck?" I asked.

"He said to come in on Monday and work a day. If he likes me, he'll take me on," Feo responded.

"Hell yeah! That's great news!" I exclaimed.

When Monday afternoon came, I anxiously waited for Feo to come home to tell me how his first day went. As he walked through the front door, he stopped at the doorway and announced, "I'm full-time starting tomorrow!"

Hearing this news brought me so much joy...and relief. For a moment, I believed we were going to be a team on this whole financial thing. Or so I thought.

What I Learned

At this point, you may be saying, *"Well, he ended up getting a job, so what's the problem?"* My issue was that he didn't do what he said he would. An unfulfilled commitment and lack of accountability from one partner can result in mistrust and leave the other person shouldering the financial responsibilities. Instead of holding himself accountable, Feo gaslit me with "how am I supposed to look for work if I don't have a car?" despite us agreeing that he would call the businesses, not drive to them. In addition, he would add "you should be grateful that I want to work. Some guys wouldn't do anything and just let you work" as a way to manipulate me and exert control.

Such behavior normalizes the person in control's inappropriate behavior against us. This emotional abuse can lead to mistrust. Following through with an action is far more important than saying what you're going to do. When you follow through, you build trust in a relationship. By not fulfilling his promise, the trust in our relationship began to suffer because this wasn't the last time Feo would not follow through.

Next Steps

Accountability is a core relationship skill needed to build trust in a relationship. When you hold your partner accountable, you are not keeping score. Instead, you are creating a safe environment for them to express themselves so that both of you can move forward. Here are a few strategies you can implement to help create a healthy environment for accountability:

- **Encourage your partner to express their feelings and perspectives.**
  - This can help you identify what their needs are and how you can support them.

- **Practice empathy**
  - This creates a safe, supportive space for them to be transparent. It is not your job to judge them, but to understand them.

- **Create a written checklist together that includes who is going to do what and when things will be done by.**
  - A checklist can be helpful because it lays out the details and fosters transparency. This leaves less room for misunderstanding or miscommunication.

- **Set up a specific time to check-in on progress instead of asking daily.**
  - This gives your partner space to make progress. During the check-in, remind each other of goals and tasks.

Having a written plan holds each person accountable and serves as a reminder of the promises made and the steps agreed upon to achieve them. More importantly, it builds trust.

Financial Mistake #5

HAVING NO FINANCIAL SAFETY NET

Navigating the early days of marriage is challenging enough, but when it's coupled with the complexities of the immigration process, the stress can be extremely overwhelming. As the sponsor and spouse of an immigrant, you may lose sight of your own financial situation because you are hyper-focused on financially taking care of the other person. You may find yourself draining your savings, putting expenses on credit cards, and accumulating far more debt than you want.

Next thing you know, you don't have a strong financial foundation anymore and you're in constant survival mode.

Once we found a place of our own, the next focus was to start working on the immigration documents for Feo. Navigating the immigration process is a long, tedious, and intricate undertaking. Any inaccuracies in the documentation can significantly set back the process.

From March 2015 through December, I diligently gathered all the necessary documents for the immigration papers, including:

- Personal information for both of us (passport, photographs, birth certificates)
- Medical records (medical examinations and vaccination record)
- Translated documents of Feo's passport and birth certificate
- Proof of current employment (pay stubs and W-2 forms)
- Most recent federal income tax return
- Information about his arrest
- Proof of cohabitation
- Photocopies of all the documents
- Speaking with an immigration attorney to ensure accuracy

I dedicated a considerable amount of energy, time, and money into completing these immigration-related tasks, while juggling a full-time job, and handling our household.

And then, there was *Daniel*.

He ended up joining us a couple months after we moved; while he looked for a job and a place to live.

"Can you look for an apartment for Daniel?" Feo requested of me. "He doesn't speak or write English well."

"I can, bu—" I responded, feeling exhausted.

"He can't stay with us forever, and he can't stay on the street. Do you want him to end up there?" Feo retorted.

"Fine, I'll help," I agreed, feeling annoyed and already overwhelmed. *Great. Another task I need to do.*

After a few weeks of contacting landlords, Daniel moved into his new place, five minutes from ours. Feo managed to get him a job at the barbershop. Daniel was around often, but it didn't bother me so much; I knew what it was like to move to a new place and not know anyone.

I let it slide. I had other tasks to focus on anyway.

After months of preparation, it was finally time to mail in the first round of immigration documents: Petition for Alien Relative. On December 5, Feo and I drove to the local FedEx. As we sat in the car, I stared at the bulky, stuffed manila envelope containing all the signed immigration documents and paperwork I had diligently compiled over the past ten months. I felt anxious as I clutched the manila envelope; but looked at Feo and gently smiled at him. "Let's do this."

Together, we stepped out of the car and walked into FedEx. I approached the sales associate and handed over what felt like the weight of the world. Finally, this burden I had been carrying for almost a year had been lifted off my shoulders. Little did I know that within 24 hours, the world and life I had known would come crashing down.

That night, we went out to dinner to celebrate. During the drive home, Feo nonchalantly mentioned he planned to continue the celebration with Daniel.

"We came to this country together. I want to celebrate with my friend. You understand, right?"

Reluctantly, I told him, "Yes." But I couldn't quite wrap my head around this comment and needed more time to process why he didn't want to celebrate together. Instead of asking him if I could join or expressing my desire to join, I let my pride and fear get in the way. Afterall, if he wanted me there, he would willingly invite me, right?

I drove him to the subway station. As I said goodbye to him, I smiled and said "Have fun. We did it."

Then I went home.

Alone.

Upset over the night, I opted to go to bed early.

Around 1 am, I woke up to use the bathroom. As I rolled over in bed, I noticed Feo wasn't there. I looked around the apartment, but I did not see him. I decided to call him out of worry. What if something had happened? The worst outcomes flooded my mind.

I called him, but all I got was the ringback tone followed by his voicemail. I called again, but got the same result—no answer. My worry grew so I decided to text him. I waited 15 minutes for a reply before deciding to go back to bed. Despite returning to bed, I found myself tossing and turning with my thoughts racing in my mind. Two hours passed and I still hadn't heard from him. My worry grew greater. I tried calling Daniel but he didn't answer either. I called Feo again, but this time it rang twice before going to voicemail.

"Did you just ignore my call?" I stared at the screen in disbelief. Irritated, I texted him and to my surprise—he turned off timestamp notifications, which would allow me to see when he read my texts.

A huge wave of unease settled in, and I knew that something was wrong. Strangely, my gut was telling me that he was safe, but up to no good. Overwhelmed with anger and helplessness, I called Kali and Jules separately to express my concerns and ask for advice. While they both thought Feo's behavior was strange, they also suggested that maybe there might be a reasonable explanation.

"There will be an explanation," Jules said. "You can't change things right now. Try to get some sleep."

At 5:31am, I received this exact text message from Feo:

"Baby haha dje sorry im drunk im sleeping at Pierre s palce. He is sleep ing i have a headache so i call you tomorrow baby sorry. I was sleeping I went to te bathrom but i have a strong headache but im really okay just wanna sleep. Sorry i did not mean to worry uou please"

A response!

I immediately called him, but once again, there was no answer. For as long as I had known Feo, he had a strong disinterest in drinking alcohol. I could count on one hand the number of times I had seen him drink and it was never to a point of inebriation. When we went out to bars or restaurants, he ordered water or soda. In fact, he often made judgemental comments about people who drank at all—including myself. So, to hear that he was drunk raised a red flag for me. The second red flag was that he was sleeping at Pierre's.

Who's Pierre? His name wasn't familiar. At this point, everything started to seem weird. Feo's unrecognizable behavior seemed out of character and I felt uneasy about it.

Feo then responded:

"I have 3% let me calm Uber i can not sleep with you texting so many times making me feel under pressure"

My response was quick. I tried not to let my fury show through it. "Just stay at whoever's place you're at. Don't call Uber. If you could sleep through all my calls and all my messages, you can sleep now. Next time please be considerate and let me know if you're going to stay at someone's place."

I didn't hear back from him.

Unable to go back to sleep, I spent the next few hours at war in my head, battling every negative thought that surfaced. Was this the moment the lies began to unravel? Afterall, we sent in the immigration documents, right? I immediately felt regret and anxiety in the pit of my stomach. I began to question whether Feo ever loved me, and I wondered if he used me to get legal residency in the U.S. Perhaps I was overanalyzing everything. Maybe he genuinely had a bit too much to drink. Maybe he really did spend the night at *Pierre's* place. Maybe his phone was actually at three percent and dying. This goes to show how powerful the stories we tell ourselves are. The narrative we construct becomes what we believe to be true, and in that moment, I unquestionably believed every story I told myself that night.

I eventually dozed off. Feo called around 10am. He was downstairs and needed to be let in because he didn't have his keys. I headed downstairs and when I opened the front door, I found him standing there with two coffees, one in each hand, and a smirk on his face. I could feel my face heating up and anger started to build up within me.

I turned around and quickly walked up the stairs and into our apartment. I threw myself onto the couch and waited for Feo to enter. When he did, he attempted to hand me a coffee, but as far as I was concerned, I was going to let that coffee turn ice cold.

"Where have you been? Why didn't you pick up the phone?" I blurted out. Then I noticed whitish stains on the bottom of his black t-shirt, and my heart began to race. Pointing at the stains, I asked, "What's that on your shirt?"

He looked down, shrugged, and asked, "What's what?" as he picked his shirt up, examining the whitish stains. "So how was your evening?"

"Why aren't you answering my questions? Why are you changing the subject?" I was growing increasingly angry.

He walked away from me and stepped outside onto the balcony to smoke a cigarette.

I followed him. "I don't believe you or your story. If you're telling me the truth, let me see your cell phone."

His eyes widened and he said "You can't. The battery is dead."

I was so livid. I didn't stop to think about asking Feo to plug his phone into the charger. Instead, I repeatedly told him that I didn't believe him, even though I technically didn't have proof. I couldn't explain how he happened to have just enough battery to call me when he was locked out, only for it to die seconds after. Overwhelmed with anger, anxiety and stress, my ability to think clearly and rationally was weakened.

Recognizing the need to calm down and regain my composure, I walked away and spent the remainder of the day struggling with my thoughts once again. Our interactions were minimal, and when we did speak, it escalated into tumultuous arguments with no resolution. The most unhinged aspect was that after each argument, his mood and behavior would shift. He would rapidly become sweet and complimentary. In hindsight, these compliments were more like backhanded remarks that left me questioning my reality. I went to bed that night feeling angry and uneasy.

The morning after, I was exhausted from the lack of sleep, continuous arguments and Feo's mood swings. With no appetite, I forced down a cup of black coffee before heading to work. I struggled with my work, too distracted with what was happening at home. As lunchtime approached, I made the decision to eat at home, then have my afternoon meeting from there.

Once I arrived home, I headed straight to the kitchen to heat up some leftover meatballs. From an outsider's perspective, it may seem like I sat at the kitchen table in silence, but in reality, I was sitting in the loudest place in the world—my inner thoughts. I scarfed down the meatballs and drank my water. With 15 minutes left before my meeting with my manager, I placed my dishes in the sink to deal with later and went to use the bathroom.

Feo had an annoying habit of leaving his dirty clothes on the bathroom floor despite the hamper being nearby. While in the bathroom, I noticed the clothes he wore the night before on the floor. Frustrated, I bent down to pick them up... that's when I saw a long, blonde hair in his black underwear.

For the first time in my life, I thought my heart would stop; It was pounding so fast and strong that my body couldn't handle it. I felt a tightness in my chest as I collapsed to the floor. As my head spun and my body shook uncontrollably, I reached for the sink and pulled myself up with the little strength I had left. Stumbling to the kitchen table, I grabbed my phone and began to dial, but my hands were trembling so badly that they caused my phone to fall from my grasp. After picking it up, I called again. Feo answered.

"HOW COULD YOU?! HOW FUCKING COULD YOU?!" I screamed. "YOU'RE A CHEATER. YOU SLEPT WITH SOMEONE ELSE ON THE SAME NIGHT THAT WE SENT IN YOUR DOCUMENTS."

I couldn't catch my breath.

"What are you talking about?" he calmly responded.

"I FOUND THE BLONDE HAIR ON YOUR CLOTHES. YOU'RE A CHEATER. GO FUCK YOURSELF. I WANT A DIVORCE. IT'S OVER!"

I hung up.

I don't think I'd ever cried like that before. It was such a deep, guttural, visceral cry of absolute devastation, horror, and heartbreak.

All I wanted at that moment was to disappear. As I lay on the ground, curled up and weeping, my meeting with my manager flashed in my mind. Without giving myself the time and space to comprehend what had just happened, I wiped my tears and took a few deep breaths to calm myself down. Still shaking, I logged onto my meeting with a forced smile on my face.

"Hi Justine! It's so nice to see you!" my manager cheerfully greeted me. And the day continued as if nothing ever happened.

The time between my meeting and Feo coming home was all a big blur. I struggled to wrap my head around everything. So many thoughts raced through my mind for hours.

I want a divorce.

How could he do this to me?

What did I do wrong?
Is this my fault?
Why am I so stupid?
What do I tell my parents?
Do I even tell my parents?
How much is a divorce?
Do I even have the money for it?

I rushed to my computer, signed into my bank account, and sighed. A couple hundred dollars in my savings stared back at me: a disheartening reminder of my financial situation. I felt defeated.

Fuck. I'm stuck.

That evening, when Feo stepped through the front door, I confronted him. With my hands shaking, I held out his black underwear containing the strand of blonde hair on it. Voice trembling, I asked "What is this?" Then I raised my voice and repeated, "What is THIS?!"

"You're crazy." He pushed past me.

My vision blurred with tears and my body heated up. "Look at it!"

Stonewalled and emotionless, he just stood there and watched me cry hysterically. When he finally walked over to look at it, he glanced at me and shrugged, "I don't see anything. You're overreacting." Then he walked away.

Once again, he tried to cast self-doubt and confusion in my mind, even with the evidence right in front of me. Exhausted from the crying and pain, I mustered up whatever energy I had left and told him, "I want a divorce."

"You're disgusting," he hissed back. "If you file for divorce, I will tell immigration that I paid you $10,000 and you will go to prison."

I wanted to scream back, but I had nothing left in me. Cheating on me was already bad enough, but trying to blackmail me with a lie, making this a transactional agreement instead of a real relationship, was just beyond hurtful. It was devastating to hear someone I thought loved me say such unkind and disrespectful things. I just sat there, alone with my thoughts.

Suffocating.

What was I going to do now?

What I Learned

My financial safety should have come first. It wasn't until something bad happened to me that I realized the importance of having a financial safety net in place *and* not giving it up to take care of someone else. You cannot provide safety to another person if you don't know how to provide safety to yourself.

Next Steps

First and foremost, take a breath. The journey you are about to embark on is going to be challenging, but it is the way to reclaim your financial freedom. The next phase of this book is dedicated to building your own financial safety net—money mindset, budgeting, saving, and debt management.

Phase 2

THE DARKNESS

My Financial Escape Plan

Leaving any relationship is hard, especially one where you are legally bound to someone.

But do you want to know what else is hard?

Staying with someone who manipulates you.

Staying with someone who calls you offensive names.

Staying with someone who blames you for their mistakes.

Staying with someone who you can't be your authentic self with.

Staying with someone who does not hold themselves accountable.

Staying with someone who intentionally finds new ways to put you down.

Staying with someone who stonewalls everytime you want to talk about an issue.

Life can and will present us with various challenges. It's up to us to choose how we deal with them.

I would be lying if I told you that I woke up the next morning and left Feo for good with my head held high. Part of me was screaming to leave because I thought I deserved better, but the other part of me clung to the belief that I was strong enough to work through the distrust and disrespect.

"He'll change," I told myself. "We *will* figure this out."

Adding to the complexity of these conflicting thoughts, I was deeply worried that I would be labeled a *divorcée* and bring shame to my family.

After a few weeks of grappling with my emotions and indecision, I gathered whatever courage and little self-belief I had left, and declared, *Enough is enough.* Recognizing it wasn't my job to change who Feo was, and acknowledging the unlikelihood of Feo changing, I redirected my energy to developing and implementing a financial safety net for myself.

This net would serve as the foundation of my plan to leave Feo. In order to start this process, I concentrated on the two aspects within my control: my attitude and my actions.

My Attitude

To be able to leave my marriage, I needed to figure out exactly what I needed, and how I would get it. Despite being the breadwinner, my financial literacy skills were lacking. My understanding was limited to saving and paying the minimum on credit cards and student loans—practices I executed poorly. I could have wallowed and beat myself up for what I didn't know and mistakes I made in the past, but that kind of attitude wasn't going to change my situation for the better. My energy and time needed to go towards me instead of going towards trying to change Feo.

So I changed my attitude; not the dude.

This shifted the focus to me. Subpar wasn't going to cut it if I wanted out. I didn't want to be the victim anymore. I wanted to become the hero of my own story.

The first hard truth I had to face as a hero was that I needed to establish security for myself. Creating this sense of security meant that I needed to straighten out my financial situation. According to the National Coalition Against

Domestic Violence, "up to ninety-nine percent of domestic violence victims experience economic abuse during their relationship, and finances are often cited as the biggest barrier to leaving."

While I hadn't experienced physical abuse yet, I had been dealing with emotional and psychological abuse from Feo for a while. Understanding the gravity of my financial situation, I decided to make the intentional decision to take control of my financial well-being as the first crucial step towards leaving this marriage.

My Actions

Would you jump if you knew there was a safety net *you* built to catch you?

Imagine a net being drawn and secured by four separate corners. When pulled evenly and tightly from all four corners, the net becomes strong enough to catch whatever falls onto it. In order to create a financial safety net for myself, I focused on rebuilding and strengthening these four financial corners:

- Money Mindset
- Budgeting
- Saving
- Debt Management

If one corner lacks the necessary tension and secure fastening, the net becomes compromised. Right now, you likely have a compromised net. Not to worry, that's what the next four chapters are for! We're going to dive deep into each of these essential financial corners and learn the necessary skills needed to pull all four corners of your financial safety net taut.

Not only will you have built this on your own, but you'll have the confidence needed to reclaim your financial autonomy. There will be a lot of information to take in, so grab your notebook, or download the free workbook at www.justinedeperalta.com/girljump and bring a positive attitude and open mind. Let's get ready to jump!

7

Corner #1

MONEY MINDSET

I'm going to say something to you that's going to sound crazy. Are you ready?

You can and *are* deserving to *rewrite* your money story.

You may be tempted to stay in the past, beating yourself up for every mistake you made, but the truth is that you can't change what happened; however, you can change what happens *now*. When it comes to rewriting your story, you can rewrite some of it or all of it. It's up to you. The stories we tell ourselves shape our realities, but aren't set in stone.

At the forefront of my financial transformation was a fundamental shift in my perspective of money. Changing how I viewed money would not be easy, but was non-negotiable if I wanted my relationship with money to be healthier. That meant I had to face three hard truths:

1. Forgive myself for my past financial mistakes. Being human involves making mistakes. They're not failures, but valuable lessons meant to be an integral part of life's journey.

2. Recognizing what I didn't know is not an indication of my future. Just because I've struggled with money before doesn't mean I always will.
3. Learn how to *unlearn*. For me to *be* someone different, I needed to *do* something different.

I dug deep into my relationship with money and where my money beliefs started. I'm sure my childhood upbringing and environment played an impressionable role on how I viewed money. Then, during my marriage, I *hated* talking about money, especially with Feo. If the topic of money came up, I would deflect or respond with a defensive "money is the root of all evil."

Feo was the opposite. He loved discussing money, but only when it was *his* money, and only on *his* terms. One night, he casually laid his cash out on our kitchen table and bragged about how much he made. The incessant talk about money and how much more money he wanted left me feeling repulsed.

For some spouses, the news of their partner making more money might be something to be excited about. For me, I was repulsed. Shortly after we moved to the North Coast, Feo started going to a local 24-hour card club to play poker. He went multiple times a week and spent hours there. Sometimes, he would come home in the wee hours of the morning pissed off because he had lost so much money. Most of the money Feo brought in went towards his gambling habit, not towards building a life together.

Other than his frivolous spending on poker, what bothered me the most was the money he spent on me after we argued. No sincere apologies, no accountability for his hurtful actions. Instead, he believed that lavish dinners and fancy outings would somehow make up for his bad behavior.

His attempts to buy my affection left me feeling furious, especially after I caught him cheating.

It took infidelity and desperation for me to want to escape and teach me this very important lesson—money isn't the *root of all evil*; it was the *tool* needed for my freedom.

As I adopted this fresh perspective, I shed all of my worn-out mantras that defined my view of money: *money is the root of all evil, money doesn't buy happiness*, and *I'm not good at money.* I let all that shit go. Instead, I rephrased the way I spoke about money by associating it with positive language.

Money = Safety
Money = Security
Money = Freedom

It was the most conscious decision I had made in the past year. I felt empowered to move forward...slowly...starting with my money mindset.

Changing my money mindset was not easy. In fact, it was challenging and scary as hell. However, every time I thought about quitting, I reminded myself that staying married to Feo was even scarier and unsafe. So I convinced myself that making these drastic changes was not only necessary, but doable.

With consistent work and mindful intention, you can gradually shift your perspective on money one day at a time by implementing this three-part strategy.

Part 1: Identify Your Money Script

Transformation begins by first identifying your *money script*. These are deeply-ingrained beliefs and narratives about money, formed early in life. There are four types of money scripts:

- **Money Avoidance**
  - When someone ignores their finances in order to avoid emotional discomfort.
  - Common phrases associated:
    - Money is bad
    - Money is the root of evil
    - It's selfish to focus on wealth
    - I avoid looking at my bank statements
    - Financial success isn't important to me
    - I get anxious so I prefer not to think about my finances

- **Money Worship**
  - When someone believes that more money will lead to greater happiness.
  - Common phrases associated:
    - Money can buy happiness
    - Money solves all problems
    - The more money, the better
    - I need more money to be fulfilled
    - Without money, life is meaningless
    - With enough money, I can handle anything

- **Money Status**
  - When someone believes that money is directly tied to their self-worth, but doesn't bring happiness. People with a money status mindset may feel the need to buy the latest Rolex and drive the most expensive car to feel valued.
  - Common phrases associated:

- I don't want people to think I'm poor
- My worth is determined by my net worth
- I can't afford to miss out on the latest trends
- If I wear designer clothes, I know I've made it
- Financial achievements define my status in society
- I need to display my wealth to be recognized and valued

- **Money Vigilance**
  - When someone evaluates their financial habits to make sure they're hitting their goals and making informed decisions. While this is the healthiest of the four money scripts, it is possible for Money Vigilance to become negative if taken too far.
  - Common phrases associated:
    - I check my finances every month
    - Financial security is a top priority for me
    - I value the peace of mind of financial stability
    - I track my spending so I know where my money is going
    - I consider the long-term consequences of my financial decisions
    - It is important to be cautious and intentional with financial decisions

Do any of these money scripts resonate with you? If you're unsure what your money script is, here are some questions you can ask yourself:

- Have you experienced a significant financial event that changed your perception of money?
- Are you happy with your relationship with money right now? Why or why not?
- What emotions do you have when someone talks to you about money?
- How often do you check your bank accounts daily? Weekly? Monthly?
- What were money conversations like while you were growing up?
- Is prioritizing an outward display of wealth important to you?
- Did you grow up talking about money with your family?
- How would you describe your attitude towards money?
- What was your earliest childhood memory of money?
- Would your life be better if you had more money?
- What are your thoughts around wealthy people?
- How do you navigate a financial issue?

Set time aside and find a place that has little to no distractions. I recommend journaling or typing out your answers to each question. Keep your responses in a place where you can easily access them. It's good practice to see where you started and track the progress you've made! As you answer these questions, be intentional and honest with yourself. By reflecting on these questions, you can gain valuable insights into your money script and start making changes towards a healthier relationship with money.

Part 2: Determining Your Current Why

When our partner cheats, our natural inclination is to seek understanding by questioning their motives. We tell ourselves, "If I just know *why* they did it, I can move on."

We may want the answers to questions like, "Why did they cheat on me?" "Why did this person use me?" "Why did this person call me demeaning names?" However, when we're in the process of survival, there is *no* luxury of time to unpack their Why. By prioritizing their Why, instead of our own, we risk losing sight of our own agency and well-being. This diminishes our own power because we're reacting to what their answer will be.

In order for you to reclaim your agency and power, you need to stop looking for *their* Why and start focusing on *yours.*

Determining your Why is the most important decision you will make on your journey. Period. Your Why becomes your driving force when shit gets tough. And trust me, *it will get tough.* There will be moments when you want to give up, distractions that sneakily or blatantly attempt to derail you, and times when you don't believe you deserve financial freedom. This is where your Why acts as an anchor and holds you to your new mindset.

For many people, knowing their Why serves as a powerful motivator for change. When I discovered that Feo had cheated on me, my life plunged into total chaos. This is going to sound surreal, but despite living in chaos, I wasn't ready to leave my marriage. Yes, I made the decision to get my finances in order, but I was still grappling with the shame that I was going to bring upon my family and myself. As a result, I initially wanted to make things work with him.

Several months later, on my lunch break at work, I logged onto what I thought was my Facebook account. To my surprise, everything was in Spanish. Initially thinking that I had previously changed the language for Spanish practice, something I often did, I proceeded to look at my messages. As I opened my inbox, my heart started to race. I stumbled upon hundreds of Facebook messages of Feo reaching out to multiple women, attempting to arrange dates while hiding his marital status. Then it hit me—I wasn't in my Facebook account, I was in Feo's.

After a moment of panic, I began to screenshot several of the messages to keep as proof. Despite having physical proof of his infidelity, I wanted confirmation from the women because I knew I wasn't going to get the truth from Feo. I decided to message some of the ladies he had been recently in contact with, introducing myself as Feo's wife and asking if they knew about me, before hastily logging out of my laptop.

I didn't have high expectations of them responding, but I felt compelled to try. To my surprise, one of them wrote back a few hours later. "Girl, you need to leave him. He told me that you were his girlfriend, not his wife. He said that you didn't live here and that you would visit from out of town." She went on to tell me that he had tried to meet up with her several times, but she thought it was weird that he had a girlfriend but was trying to meet other women. "He doesn't deserve you. I'm so sorry."

I was overwhelmed with gratitude for that woman's kindness and courage. She didn't owe me an explanation. She had no obligation to me, yet she took the time to send me a compassionate response. Deep down inside, I knew this wasn't about the other woman, and it was no longer about Feo. It was about *me* now and the decisions I needed to make towards reclaiming my safety and well-being. That was my new Why.

Determining your Why involves self-reflection and understanding of your values. It can be challenging to uncover what your Why is, so here is a three-step exercise on how to determine your current Why:

1. Brainstorm
- O Grab a pen and paper (or use your preferred method). Start by asking yourself, "What is my 'why' right now?" Turn on a timer for 10 minutes then begin to write down anything that comes to mind. It could be words, phrases, feelings, beliefs, values, and passions.

<u>What is my "why" right now?</u>

Full of anger and resenment   Cheated on me

I don't want to be in married   Unhappy

Desperation   We are very different

Gaslighting
Don't share same values

Exhausted
Fear for my life
Unhealthy/toxic
Stressed
No transparency

Making unhealthy choices
Spinning out of control
Losing sense of self

2. Dig Deeper
- O Once time is up, select one of your initial answers and ask yourself, "Why is this important to me right now?" Write down your honest response. Repeat this question after

each new response. This will encourage you to explore deeper layers of your purpose.

3. Get to the Root
- ○ Repeat this process until you no longer have anything left to say. This signifies you've unearthed the core root of your current Why.

<u>**Cheated on me**</u>

"Why is this important to me right now?"
I don't want to be with someone who cheats on me

"Why is this important to me right now?"
There is no loyalty

"Why is this important to me right now?"
I don't trust this person

"Why is this important to me right now?"
I don't want to be with a person I don't trust

"Why is this important to me right now?"
If I can't trust you , I don't feel safe and I make bad decisions

"Why is this important to me right now?"
I value my safety and well-being

At the end of the exercise, my current Why was reclaiming my overall safety and well-being.

While your Why can change and evolve overtime, it's important to stick to the one that keeps you on track and gets you closer to a more meaningful life. If you change your Why frequently, you may find yourself not achieving the progress you want.

Without a Why, you don't have clarity on what your next steps will be.

Without a Why, you can struggle to move forward.

Without a Why, you stay in chaos.

Part 3: Make an Intentional Decision

Now that you've identified your Why, the next crucial step is making an intentional decision based on your Why. Moving forward, every action and decision will be focused on your Why. Decision-making while living through chaos can feel overwhelming and daunting, especially when you may not know where to begin. To determine which decision to act on first, you'll need to unpack your needs following these four steps:

1. **Write your Why at the top of a piece of paper.**
   - For me, my Why was my safety.

2. **Ask yourself, "In order for me to have <u>A,</u> I need to <u>B</u>."**
   - In order for me to <u>have safety,</u> I need <u>to leave my marriage.</u>

3. **Then unpack further.**
   - In order for me to <u>leave my marriage</u>, I need <u>money to move out and file for divorce.</u>

4. **Continue this process until you reach a specific, tangible task you can take.**
   - In order for me to <u>have the money to move out and file for divorce</u>, I need <u>to figure out how much money it would take for me to do that.</u>
   - In order for me to <u>figure out how much money I need,</u> I need <u>to see how much money I have.</u>
   - In order for me to <u>see how much money I have,</u> I need to create a budget.

By using the framework "In order for me to _____, I need to _____," you can gain a clearer understanding of what is *exactly* needed to make an intentional decision. By making intentional decisions, we recognize and gain greater clarity on what truly matters to us, even in the midst of chaos.

For me — I value safety. In order to achieve financial and emotional security, I would need to create a budget that prioritized saving and debt management.

At the end of the day, you don't need perfection or a complete understanding to take action. Embracing the mindset of needing to know one percent more than the day before is sufficient to take the next step. It's okay to make mistakes. What's important is that you learn from those mistakes; and move forward. Perfection won't save your life. Progress from action will.

Change your mindset. Change your story.

Next Steps

Follow the checklist below to get started.

- ☐ **Identify your money scripts**
  - ○ Set aside time to have an honest conversation with yourself about the money scripts you currently identify with and how you plan to change them

- ☐ **Determine your Why**
  - ○ Brainstorm
  - ○ Dig deep
  - ○ Get to the root

- ☐ **Start making intentional decisions based on your Why**

8
Corner #2

A WORKABLE BUDGET

In Chapter 7, we dove into the importance of identifying your money mindset in order to start rewriting your story. Now, it's time to focus on the second corner of your financial safety net: *budgeting*. If you just rolled your eyes, or panic set in because you just read the word *budget*, I completely understand. It's not the sexiest word in the dictionary, but being trapped in an abusive relationship isn't any more appealing. I'm here to gently remind you that this journey won't be a walk in the park, but it is absolutely doable.

You are going to apply these concepts to how you view a budget and what a budget means to you. If renaming it to something like "Financial Escape Plan" or even the "Fuck this, I'm out!" plan sparks enthusiasm in managing your money, then do it! Changing your perspective on what you call a budget is a crucial step towards motivating yourself to take proactive action towards your financial goals.

What is a budget and why is it important to have one?

A *budget* is a finance plan that allocates future personal income toward expenses, savings, debt repayment, and investing. Having a budget in place allows you to easily track your income and expenses, which will allow you to save money and pay down bad debt more easily and efficiently. More importantly, a budget identifies exactly where each of your dollars goes. *You* have the control to tell each dollar where to go! Knowing where your money comes from and where your money goes can give you confidence and help you build a more secure financial future.

As you begin your budgeting journey, concentrate on these three key priorities to set a strong foundation for effectively managing your finances:

- Set realistic and manageable goals
- Prioritize expenses that are *needs,* not *wants*
- Allocate a portion of your income to savings and debt management

Your objective is to focus on *your* results. To achieve the results *you* desire, you must spend on what you value *and* is crucial to your survival.

Creating a Workable and Sustainable Budget

Creating a workable and sustainable budget can be done with clear steps in place. Here are five steps for creating a workable budget that align with your goals and Why.

Step 1: Determine monthly income

Any money you earn from a range of sources counts as income. You may receive income from:

- **Wages and Salary**
  - This is money you earn from your job. Your take-home income is the money you receive after

taxes, benefits, and voluntary contributions from a paycheck.

- **Commission**
  - This is money that is earned for completing a task. This usually comes from selling a certain amount of products and/or services. This form of income may vary month to month, so keep that in mind.

- **Side hustles/gigs**
  - This is extra money outside of your main source of income. This form of income may vary month to month.

- **Government Benefits**
  - This is money or monetary value given by the government for financial assistance. This includes food assistance, Social Security, housing help, welfare, health insurance, and disability.

- **Gifts**
  - This is money that is given to you unexpectedly or one-time. While this is a type of income to be grateful for, it is not something to rely on.

- **Allowance**
  - This is a set amount of money given to you on a recurring basis. Allowance can typically be given to you from a spouse, family member, or employer. This money can be used for common expenses. You can even put some of this money into your savings.

If you currently have no income, ask for help from trusted family members and friends. Given the delicate nature of this situation, it's important to approach it with clarity and respect. Be clear and honest about your needs, and ask if they are willing to provide any monetary assistance. Offer a repayment plan that works for both of you. If they are unwilling, express gratitude then try requesting gift cards.

Gift cards can help you make ends meet and afford basic needs such as food, housing, transportation, clothes, toiletries, and proper healthcare. They offer practical and immediate assistance. Here are some of the types of gift cards you can request:

- Retailers
- Pharmacies
- Supermarkets
- Transportation
- Clothing Stores
- Prepaid cards

If your friends and family members are still unable to help, you can reach out to a local shelter or family justice center. Many of these shelters and centers provide free services, including legal aid and financial services. You can also contact the Domestic Violence Hotline at (800) 799-SAFE (7233) and speak with an advocate who can refer you to financial services.

Step 2: Calculate SURVIVAL expenses

Expenses are outgoing funds you pay to others. Before calculating what your survival expenses are, it's important to first understand what the three types of expenses are—Fixed, Variable, and Periodic.

- **Fixed:** These are expenses that remain the same each month.
  - Rent
  - Internet
  - Phone bill
  - Loan payments
  - Mortgage payment
  - Insurance premiums
  - Subscription services

- **Variable:** These are expenses that may change from month-to-month.
  - Gas
  - Groceries
  - Utility bills
  - Dining out
  - Entertainment
  - Transportation

- **Periodic:** These are expenses that do not occur monthly, but happen sporadically throughout the year.
  - Property taxes
  - Holiday expenses
  - Vehicle registration
  - Insurance premiums
  - Annual subscriptions

All three of these expenses will be a part of your budget. The key is to prioritize your needs from your wants. A *need* is something you must have for survival. For this reason, I call the *needs* expenses as "survival expenses." These are examples of survival expenses to prioritize:

- **Rent/Mortgage**
  - This monthly payment provides a roof over your head!

- **Utilities**
  - These include basic climate control, electricity, and running water.

- **Transportation**
  - Depending on where you live, you may need a transit card, bike, car and gas to earn income. You may also need this for your safety.

- **Groceries**
  - Buying food that supports your health. This does not include expensive dinners and poor nutritional choices.

- **Affordable clothing**
  - This is clothing that is comfortable and appropriate for whatever you have to do. This doesn't include designer clothes or additional clothing.

A *want* is something you would like to have, but is not necessary for your survival. Examples of *wants* can include designer clothes, new phones, vacations, jewelry, entertainment, and dining out. There are several factors such as advertising, peers, influencers, family, and personal experiences that influence your desire to buy *wants.* Depending on an individual's situation, needs and wants will vary greatly.

Once fixed and variable expenses have been calculated, the next step is to determine what money is leftover, if any, for savings and debt repayment.

Step 3: Determine leftover money

To determine how much money you have left after covering your expenses, you will need to subtract your expenses from your income. If you don't have any money leftover, this indicates you are living above your means. When you live above your means, you are spending more than you earn. Ideally, the goal is to live below your means, signifying that you spend less than you earn.

If you find yourself with no money leftover after you've subtracted your survival expenses from your monthly income, you'll need to find ways to reduce your current expenses. Consider these actionable steps:

- Stop, sell, or cancel anything that is not considered a need
- Look for discounts and sales when shopping for essentials
- Cancel any subscriptions that can lead to spending more
- Learn to say *no* to what doesn't serve your goal
- Create a grocery shopping list and stick to it
- Negotiate utility bills to get lower rates
- Cook at home instead of eating out
- Avoid impulse buying

If you still don't have money leftover even after trimming expenses, it may be a good idea to look into ways you can increase your income. Remember this—there's a limit as to how much you can trim expenses, but there's no limit to your earning potential. Here are some ways you can increase your income:

- Negotiate a higher salary or seek out advancement opportunities within your workplace
- Explore part-time jobs that align with your interests and abilities
- Sell items in your home that you no longer need
- Participate in online focus groups and surveys
- Create and sell products online or in-person
- Offer freelancing or consulting services
- Rent out personal equipment

During this challenging time, I encourage you to invest in your continued learning. If possible, try to enroll in free training programs or courses that can help improve your skills. Online platforms such as Coursera and edX provide a variety of standalone courses from their learning pathways and multiple educational partners. Listen to podcasts and audiobooks. If you have a library card, you can read ebooks and listen to audiobooks from mobile apps such as Libby and Hoopla. Having a diverse skill set can help increase employability and open up new job opportunities. If you're unsure where to go, seek out help from local government agencies and organizations that support domestic violence victims. They can guide you towards training programs and education tailored to your needs and circumstances.

Step 4: Allocate leftover money to savings and debt repayment

You may be tempted to go on a shopping spree or spend money at the bar as ways to escape reality. While these actions may bring happiness in the moment, they can bring you more guilt and shame in the long run.

Creating a budget that prioritizes savings and debt repayment is the foundation of your financial safety net. By focusing on saving and debt repayment, you build financial stability for yourself and create peace of mind.

Step 5: Take action NOW

After you've created your budget, the next crucial step is to take action *now*. Ask yourself these questions to see if you are on track and to identify what you need to take action on:

- Are you living below your means?
- Have you cut down on unnecessary expenses?
- Are you able to log into your banking accounts?
- Are you contributing to your emergency fund regularly?
- Are you paying at least the minimum on your monthly credit card payments?
- Have you viewed your free annual credit report from annualcreditreport.com?

Regularly monitoring your spending can improve your financial literacy and provide peace of mind because you have a clearer understanding of your financial situation. More importantly, you build the confidence to advocate for yourself and make informed financial decisions that support your goals. If your first attempts at a budget don't quite go according to plan, don't give up. Budgeting isn't something that is set in stone. It is meant to be adjusted in order to align with your financial goals and put you in a position of making important financial decisions.

Next Steps

Follow the checklist below to get started.

- ☐ **Determine monthly income**
  - ○ Where is your money coming from?
  - ○ How much money do you make every month?

- ☐ **Calculate survival expenses**
  - ○ Rent/Mortgage
  - ○ Utilities
  - ○ Transportation
  - ○ Groceries
  - ○ Affordable clothing

- ☐ **Determine leftover money**
  - ○ If you don't have leftover money or much of it, consider cutting down on unnecessary expenses and/or increase your income

- ☐ **Put leftover money towards savings and debt repayment**

- ☐ **Regularly monitor spending**
  - ○ Pick a date to check in on your budget and make adjustments accordingly

9
Corner #3

AN EMERGENCY FUND

With the first two corners established, let's shift our focus to the third corner: savings. When it comes to a savings plan, there are three components: emergency fund, short-term and long-term savings. While all three are important, the emergency fund takes precedence. The main reason behind prioritizing an emergency fund over short-term and long-term savings is liquidity. You want to be able to access this money easily. Having an emergency fund is important because you may experience an unexpected event that requires a substantial amount of money. In such instances, your emergency fund serves as the primary source of financial support. If possible, avoid using credit cards in emergency situations to prevent further accumulation of debt. We'll talk more about debt in the next chapter.

What counts as an emergency? Here are examples of expenses an emergency fund could be used for:

- **Family emergencies**
  - Flight home due to the sudden loss or health of a family member.

- **Medical emergencies**
  - Cutting finger open while slicing Christmas ham.

- **Critical home or vehicle repairs**
  - The roof has a leak.

Here are some examples of what your emergency fund should NOT be used for:

- Investments
- Impulse splurges
- Bills you cannot afford
- Plannable annual expenses
- Unnecessary home renovations
- Vacations, day trips, or road trips
- Brunch on the weekends with friends

Before you start funding your emergency fund, you'll want to calculate how much to save. A popular budgeting framework created by Senator Elizabeth Warren is the 50/30/20 rule where:

- 50% of your budget goes towards *needs*
- 30% of your budget goes towards *wants*
- 20% of your budget goes towards *savings* and *debt repayment*

With that being said, the ideal percentage for savings can vary based on an individual's situation and goals. If you're looking to pay off debt faster, you may want to decrease your *wants* expenses and put that extra money towards debt repayment. If you want to build your emergency fund as quickly as possible, you may allocate more money towards savings. With your budget in place, you should know how much money you have left after expenses. With whatever you have left, allocate some of it towards your emergency fund. Ideally, the goal is to save between 3 to 6 months' worth of expenses.

If possible, put aside ten percent of your income towards your emergency fund. If you are unable to put this amount aside, that's okay. Start small. It could be $5 or $10. You can add more in the future. The point is to start so that you have *something* instead of nothing. A great way for you to know if you're on track with your savings is by calculating your *Savings Rate* or *Savings Ratio*. To calculate your savings rate, you take the sum of your monthly expenses and divide it by your monthly net income.

Here is an example:

A	B
Monthly Expenses = $4,000	Monthly Expenses = $2,500
Monthly Net Income = $5,000	Monthly Net Income = $2,000
$4,000 / $5,000 = .8	$2,500 / $2,000 = 1.25
1.0 - 0.8 = 0.2 or *20%*	1.0 -1.25 = -0.25 or *-25%*

The goal is to have at least a 20% or higher savings rate. The higher the savings rate, the better!

Remember—the primary purpose of your emergency fund is to *save* money. If you find yourself getting distracted from the goal of saving money, take a deep breath and revisit your Why.

Creating and Funding An Emergency Fund

Creating and funding an emergency fund sounds daunting, but if you have clear steps in place, you can start today. To get started with saving, here are five steps for creating and funding an emergency fund.

Step 1: Choose a Bank Institution

There are several financial institutions to choose from. As you shop around, you may come across the most common institutions—banks and credit unions. Banks and credit unions offer a variety of services. Some of the most common are:

- **Checking and Savings Accounts**
  - You can store and manage your money in these accounts. A *checking account* is the account where most of your day-to-day transactions take place. This is where your paychecks and income are deposited and where your bill payments and transfers to other accounts happen.
  - A *savings account* is where you deposit your money for your emergency fund, short-term savings, and long-term savings. With a savings account, you want to avoid pulling out money unless the money is going to be used for the intended purpose of the savings fund.

- **Online and Mobile Banking**
  - You can manage your bank accounts online without having to go in-person.

- **Automated Teller Machine (ATM) Services**
  - You can withdraw cash from accessible ATMs. You can locate the nearest ATM via the banking app or online.

- **Wire Transfers**
  - You can electronically send and receive money from a person or institution. This can be a domestic or international transfer.

- **Safety Deposit Boxes**
  - You can store valuable items or important documents in a safety deposit box.

- **Debit and Credit Cards**
  - A *debit card* is directly linked to a checking account. When a transaction takes place, the money is automatically withdrawn from that account. The money in this account is the user's own money.
  - A *credit card* allows users to make purchases using borrowed money from the bank. Since the card lender is lending the user money, they charge interest each month until the entire balance is paid. When it comes to loans and bad debt, interest on your money does NOT work in favor of you. Depending on what your outstanding balance is and annual percentage rate (APR), you can end up paying more than what you originally spent if you don't pay in full your credit card debt each month.

- **Loans**

- You can take out a personal loan, auto loan, and mortgage.

- **Financial Education**
  - Some banks and credit unions provide free financial education resources and workshops to help customers with their financial literacy.

While banks and credit unions provide similar services, they have different benefits and terms. So it's important to understand what these differences are before deciding which is best for you.

Here are a few factors to keep in mind when choosing a financial institution:

- **FDIC insured**
  - This deposit insurance protects your money in the event of a bank failure.

- **No minimum monthly balance**
  - Some checking and savings accounts require you to have a certain amount of money in order to avoid monthly fees. An account that doesn't require a minimum balance can help you avoid extra charges.

- **No monthly maintenance fees**
  - Some banks charge a monthly maintenance fee. This is a charge you pay each month for having a checking and/or savings account with their institution.

- **No minimum opening deposit**
  - Some financial institutions may require a minimum dollar amount when opening an

account. If possible, look for accounts that do not require a minimum opening balance.

- **Pays you interest**
  - When it comes to your checking and savings accounts, interest is your friend! Savings accounts generally have a Savings Interest Rate called the annual percentage yield. This is a percentage rate that you earn based on your account balance. In other words, the financial institution pays you every month for depositing your cash in their savings accounts. As of Feb 2024, the *average annual percentage yield* (APY) for savings accounts is .58%. With that being said, online savings accounts can offer 4.5% or higher. The interest rates vary based on account options, financial institution, and how much money you have in your account. As for checking accounts, there are some institutions who offer interest rates on checking accounts but these are limited. At the end of the day, earning interest on your banking accounts allows you to grow your money over time with the help of compound interest. The higher the APY, the more money you'll earn over time!

- **Direct Deposit**
  - If you are currently working and have the option of Direct Deposit, have your employer directly deposit your paycheck into your account every pay period. This is safer than receiving a paper check because the money goes directly into your checking and/or savings accounts. If your employer doesn't offer direct deposit, that's

okay. While having direct deposit is a benefit, it is not a necessity when opening a bank account.

- **Bill Pay and Automation**
  - Instead of manually paying your bills, you can set up your online banking to automatically pay all your bills each month. When you set up automatic bill pay properly, you can avoid any late fees and protect your credit by ensuring that all your bills are paid on time each month. Additionally, you can automate your savings. By putting money aside for savings, you are "paying yourself first." Automation can help improve your credit score, contribute to your emergency fund, relieve financial stress, and redirect your time and focus on other important matters.

- **Confidentiality**
  - Request your contact information be confidential and secure. This could mean omitting addresses from external documents, adding an additional layer of verification, and confirmation that contact information is safe. Banks are legally required to protect the privacy of their customers.

- **Convenience**
  - Convenience is an important factor to consider when choosing a financial institution. Is the bank physically close by? Do you have access to online and mobile banking? Is it easy to deposit money? Are there ATMs located nearby? Can

you access your money easily and efficiently? Convenience can make it easy for you to manage and access your money wherever you are.

Take your time as you review the pros and cons of each financial institution. Building a strong relationship with your financial institution can pay off in the future because who you decide to go with can help you successfully reach your financial goals.

Step 2: Gather all necessary documents

Specific information and documentation may vary from financial institution, but here are the common documents needed to open checking and savings accounts:

- **A valid government-issued ID**
  - ○ This can include a valid passport, passport card, driver's license, other government-issued ID, military card.

- **Social Security Number (SSN) or Individual Tax Identification Number (ITIN)**
  - ○ If you do not have a Social Security Number, you can apply for an Individual Tax Identification Number (ITIN) at www.irs.gov. The application process is free. If you're worried about your privacy due to your immigration status, there are laws in place preventing the IRS from sharing your personal information with other governmental agencies.

- **Contact information**
  - This includes a phone number and email address.

- **Date of birth**

- **Proof of current address and possibly former addressed**
  - This can be a utility bill, rental agreement, internet or cable bill.

- **Initial deposit**
  - As mentioned previously, you'll want to look for a financial institution that offers no minimum opening deposit. This is different from the initial investment. The initial investment is the amount you choose to deposit when opening an account, even if there is no minimum opening deposit required by the financial institution. For example, Bank ABC doesn't require a minimum opening deposit so you decided to put in $5 as your initial deposit. Meanwhile, Bank CBA requires $300 as a minimum opening deposit so you decide not to go with them.

Once you've gathered all necessary documents and information, it's time to choose a savings account to hold your emergency fund.

Step 3: Choose your Savings account

While you can keep money in a checking and savings account, a savings account can help you save money faster for two reasons:

- **Higher interest rates**
  - Interest rates typically offered on savings accounts are higher in comparison to checking accounts. Although there are checking accounts that may offer an interest rate, it tends to be lower in comparison to a savings account. The faster our money grows, the better!

- **Limit overspending**
  - Accessing money in a savings account is not as easy as checking accounts. Many savings accounts have a limit on monthly withdrawals, restricting the number of times you can access your funds. These withdrawal limits can keep you from spending money that is intended for saving.

Financial institutions offer various types of savings accounts, each with distinct features and benefits. Three common savings accounts are:

- **Traditional Savings Accounts**
  - Traditional Savings Accounts, or regular savings accounts, are the most familiar type of savings account. These accounts are available at traditional brick and mortar banks and credit unions. Money can be withdrawn easily and deposited. As of February 2024, the national average APY is .23%.

- **High-yield Savings Accounts**
  - High-yield savings accounts (HYSA) are similar to traditional savings accounts but with a higher interest rate. As of February 2024, the APY is 5.84%. These accounts are generally available online, have no monthly fees, and have low (or no) minimum balances and requirements.

- **Certificates of Deposits**
  - Certificates of Deposits (CD) are a type of savings account that earns interest over a certain time frame. Upon opening a CD, you deposit a lump sum of money that is locked in for a fixed term. If at any time you want to withdraw your money before the fixed term ends, you will be hit with penalty fees. The interest rates are higher compared to traditional savings accounts. As of February 2024, the APY is between 1.4%-1.72%, depending on how long the term is.

Each has their pros and cons, but if you're looking to grow your money faster and is not a fixed term, a high-yield savings account would be the best option.

Step 4: Open Savings Account

Nowadays, opening a bank account can be done online and doesn't require going in-person to your local financial institution. During the process, you will:

- **Select Account Type**
  - Individual
    - Account with a single account holder

- If you are married or in a relationship, you can open this account under your name only and without your significant other
  - Joint
    - Account shared between two or more account holders
    - Both account holders can access and manage money
  - Custodial
    - Account for minors that is created and managed by custodians
    - The custodian manages this account until the minor becomes of legal age

- **Enter Personal Information**
  - First Name
  - Last Name
  - Social Security or ITIN
  - Date of Birth
  - Street Address
  - Email Address
  - Phone number
  - Occupation
  - Country of citizenship

Once you submit your application, the bank will need to verify your information. Approvals take between two to five business days. Upon approval, you are ready to make your first deposit!

- **Make first deposit**
  - If you've chosen a bank account that doesn't require a minimum opening balance, you are not expected to make a deposit at this time.

However, as emphasized earlier, initiating savings early is crucial, even if the initial deposit is $5. It's in your best interest to get into the habit of adding money to your bank accounts.

o If you are working and direct deposit is offered, consider having your paychecks directly deposited into your account every pay period. Ideally, connecting direct deposit to both your checking and savings accounts could help you separate what goes towards savings and bills. However, if you're unable to do so, that's okay. It is not necessary to use direct deposit for multiple accounts. One account is sufficient.

o If you receive physical checks from your employer, many financial institutions allow users to deposit checks with eCheck deposit. If your income is cash, you have the option to deposit your cash into a separate bank account that has ATMs or branches. This requires you to have a checking account at a financial institution different from your savings account. Another option is to buy a money order at a money transfer service and make it payable to yourself. Then, you can use eCheck deposit to put the money into your online savings account.

The sooner you start funding your accounts, the faster your savings journey begins and the closer you get to achieving financial security. This is more than just saving money. This is about building the confidence needed to start a new chapter in your life.

With that said...

CONGRATULATIONS!

You've successfully and officially established your very own savings and checking accounts. Achieving this milestone wasn't easy, but YOU DID IT. **I'm so proud of you!**

Step 5: Automate Savings

The strength of your financial safety net is built on consistency. Every time you deposit money into your savings accounts, your financial security gets stronger. Automating deposits into your savings is one of the best ways to keep the momentum going because it:

- Ensures a portion of your income is consistently allocated towards savings without you manually doing it
- Lessens the stress that comes with monitoring and managing your money
- Removes temptation from spending money that was meant to be saved
- Saves you time and effort

When setting up automation, consider the following:

- **Review your budget**
  - Take a closer look at your budget and make sure you have enough money coming in and going out each month. To be on the safe side, consider leaving a buffer in your checking account to prevent potential overdrafts. This additional cushion can bring peace of

mind in the event of an unexpected financial disruption.

- **Take note of due dates and pay dates**
  - Due dates are for bills and credit card payments. Pay dates are when you receive income. If you're unsure of the due dates, reach out to each company for that information. Mark all due dates and pay dates on your calendar.
  - Once you've gathered all information, align your automatic transfers to your savings account and bill payments with your pay dates. This can ensure that money is going towards your savings and that you have the funds to make bill payments, reducing the risk of overdrafts or missed payments.

- **Set up alerts and reminders**
  - Enable alerts for each transfer and bill payment. Alerts notify you of account-related activities that may impact your finances. Alerts for low balance, direct deposit, unusual activity, large purchase, large withdrawal, and profile changes can help you take immediate action if need be.
  - Reminders, on the other hand, let you know of upcoming bill payments. On your calendar, schedule the first reminder two days before and the second the day of. This gives you a buffer time, in case you need to adjust your funds.

Feeling overwhelmed? Here are some small but mighty money moves you can make to start building your emergency fund:

- **Set small savings goals**
  - Set small tangible goals that serve as checkpoints to your larger goal. For example, if your end goal is $3000, you may want to set your first checkpoint at $50. As you work towards this first milestone, try not getting caught up in what the next small goal is. When thinking about goals in the future, you direct your energy and attention towards something that hasn't happened yet. Remember— you're more likely to get to your destination if you take small, achievable steps instead of giant, unstable leaps. Last but not least, every time you accomplish a small goal, take a moment to celebrate. Acknowledge the effort you're putting in and the promises you are keeping to yourself. That alone is a powerful accomplishment!

- **Start with small, consistent contributions**
  - Saving three months worth of expenses will not happen overnight; it takes time and consistency. Start with an amount that you can comfortably set aside each month. Over time, consider increasing your contributions as your financial situation improves. If, for any reason, you are unable to contribute the planned amount, the best thing to do is pivot and adjust accordingly. This may mean putting only $5 into savings instead of $50. At one point during my journey, I remember putting $1 into my

savings for the months that I was struggling. If you stop making contributions, restarting becomes more challenging because you lose that momentum. So, even if it's a smaller amount, your consistency built through small steps helps maintain momentum and progress. More importantly, you build the confidence to make giant financial leaps later.

You've done it! Your emergency fund is established and funded. Now it's time to set up your debt repayment plan.

Next Steps

Follow the checklist below to get started.

- ☐ **Choose bank institution**
  - ○ FDIC insured
  - ○ Has no minimum monthly balance
  - ○ Has no minimum opening deposit requirement

- ☐ **Gather all necessary documents**
  - ○ Valid government issued ID
  - ○ SSN or ITIN
  - ○ Proof of current address (utility bill, rental agreement, internet/cable bill)

- ☐ **Open Individual high yield savings account (HYSA) and checking account**

- ☐ **Deposit money into emergency fund in savings account**

- ☐ **Automate monthly deposits into emergency fund**

10
Corner #4

DEBT MANAGEMENT

When I was 18 years old, I opened my very first credit card—a Macy's store card. The cashier's offer to open a store credit card for an extra 15% off my purchase caught my attention. At the time, this seemed like a smart financial decision since I would be saving money. So, I quickly signed up. Little did I know, this simple decision came with complexities I was unaware of and I quickly learned that there's so much more to know about credit cards.

"Mom! I saved 15% on my purchase at Macy's!" I exclaimed, excited.

"Oh really? Was it on sale?"

I began to explain. "No, the cashier told me I could save 15% on my purchase if I opened up a store car—"

"Oh no! Why did you do that?!" my mother shrieked.

My mom spent the next twenty minutes explaining to me what a credit card was and the importance of always paying on time and paying at least the monthly minimum. I soaked in this information and did my best to follow her advice.

However, I am human; and despite my mom's advice and teachings, there were instances where I managed to pay the monthly minimum, but not on time. Eventually, when I did, I had to deal with the late fees and growing debt.

During my time married to Feo, I juggled nearly $10,000 in credit card debt and had a medical bill in collections. As a result, I had an abysmal credit score. Given the financial situation I was in, I knew that if I wanted to create financial security for myself, I would not only need a funded emergency savings, but I would also need to pay down my debt and boost my low credit score as fast as I could. First, I had to understand *what* exact debt I needed to pay off.

"Good debt" vs. "Bad Debt"

There are two general categories of debt—*good* debt and *bad* debt.

Good debt refers to loans that are used to purchase items that we believe will go up in value or provide a revenue stream that may increase our wealth over time. Investment, home (mortgages), business and educational loans are generally considered *good* debt.

Bad debt refers to loans used to purchase items that typically go down in value or they don't help improve your financial situation. Credit cards, auto, payday and personal loans are generally considered *bad* debt.

One thing to keep in mind is that differentiating between what is *good* and *bad* debt can get tricky because there are many variables to consider. There can be situations where your *good* debt becomes *bad* debt, such as when a home loan is on property that loses value; and your *bad* debt can become your *good* debt, such as when using a credit card to buy professional clothes, which in turn help you land a better-paying job.

A good question you can ask yourself as you unpack what kind of debt you have is "Does this debt get me closer to my financial goals or does it push me farther away?" Take note of the debt that pushes you further away. That will be the *bad* debt to focus on repaying. Your repayment plan should focus on paying down debt fastest *and* ensure your monthly credit card bills are paid on time.

Credit Score and How It Impacts You

In the United States, there are a variety of companies, each having their own scoring models, that provide credit scores—a three digit number that evaluates a borrower's ability to pay back debt. When lenders and creditors are evaluating a borrower, the most commonly used score is the FICO score. A borrower's FICO score is comprised of five categories:

- **Payment history (35%)**
  - ○ Lenders are looking at your payments and if they are made on time, everytime. If you are late on bill payments, this will negatively impact your credit score.

- **Amounts owed (30%)**
  - ○ This is your credit utilization. Lenders look at how much of your available credit you are using compared to how much total credit you have. To calculate your credit utilization, divide your total debt by your total credit . Rule of thumb is to keep your credit utilization below 30%.

- **Length of credit history (15%)**
  - Lenders want to know if you are able to manage credit responsibly over a long period of time. Closing your oldest credit account can shorten your credit history. If you want to build good credit, avoid closing your credit cards, even if you're no longer using them. To keep those cards active, you can put a small expense on them, but make sure to pay that expense in full by the due date.

- **New credit (10%)**
  - Lenders look at how many hard credit inquiries you have on your account. There are two types of credit inquiries—hard and soft. *Hard credit inquiries* are done by lenders when they check your credit and these credit checks are officially recorded on your credit report. A *soft credit inquiry* is done by you or someone you authorize to check your credit report. Soft credit inquiries do not affect your credit score. If you apply for too much credit all at once, this could negatively impact your credit score. Try waiting six months between applications instead.

- **Credit mix (10%)**
  - Lenders like to see that you have different types of credit. This includes revolving debt and installment debt. *Revolving debt* is an ongoing line of credit that you can borrow from as needed. Credit cards are an example of revolving debt. *Installment debt* is a lump sum of money given to you upfront and is

repaid through regular, fixed payments over a set period of time. Student loans and car loans are examples of installment debt. If you don't have any loans, you can still build credit with just credit cards.

A borrower's score then falls into a range that lenders look at. Here are the FICO ranges:

- 800 - 850: Exceptional
- 740 - 799: Very Good
- 670 - 739: Good
- 580 - 669: Fair
- 300 - 579: Risky

There are several benefits to having a good credit score. When you have a good credit score, you can qualify for lower interest rates when you open new loans and lines of credit. The lower the interest rate, the more money you save over time. Additionally, having good credit can help improve your chances of securing job opportunities because some employers may check credit reports as part of the hiring process. When it comes to housing, landlords and property management check credit scores as part of the screening process. Having a good credit score can increase your chances of being approved. This also applies to car buying and leasing processes. As you can see, having good credit gives you financial flexibility and stability needed to achieve your financial goals.

Unsecured vs. Secured Credit Cards

An unsecured credit card does not require a deposit as collateral. Most credit cards are unsecured; and tend to come with lower fees, lower interest rates, and better perks and rewards. Unsecured credit can help you build credit because your payments are reported to the credit bureaus. Overall, having access to unsecured credit tends to be a better deal for consumers. Qualifying for an unsecured credit card can be incredibly difficult if you have poor credit (669 and below), so the next best course of action would be applying for a secured credit card.

If your credit score is in the fair or risky range (669 or below) or you don't have an established credit history, it may be difficult to get approved for a new credit line or loan. One way you can build credit is through a secured credit card. A secured credit card is a type of credit card that requires a cash deposit as collateral. In other words, you put down a cash deposit and whatever that amount is will be how much credit you'll receive. For example, if you deposit $200 as collateral, you'll typically qualify for a $200 line of credit. Just like unsecured credit, your payments are reported to the credit bureaus, so it is important to pay your credit card bills on-time and to keep your credit utilization under 30%. This will help you build credit and improve your credit history over time.

After using your secured credit card for an extended period of time, as your credit score improves, you can request to have your secured credit card upgraded to an unsecured card.

Creating a Sustainable Debt Repayment Plan

Now that you have a better understanding of your debt and credit, it's time to create a sustainable debt repayment plan that focuses on building confidence, setting up on-time bill payments, and paying debt down quickly.

Step 1: List all debt

Before deciding on a debt repayment method, list all of your debts. Include the following:

- **Name of Lender:** Who you borrowed the money from
- **Principal Balance:** The original amount borrowed
- **Interest:** The amount you're charged on top of the principal borrowed
- **Remaining Balance:** What is left to pay
- **Minimum Monthly Payment:** The lowest amount that can be paid to remain in good standing.

Here is an example:

Name of Lender	Principal Balance	Interest	Remaining Balance	Minimum Monthly Payment
Credit Card #1	$5,000	21.89%	$2,000	$45
Credit Card #2	$4,000	19.84%	$1,000	$40
Credit Card #3	$8,000	20.99%	$7,000	$210
Student Loan #1	$80,000	6.625%	$69,000	$500
Auto Loan #1	$25,000	6.63%	$20,000	$480
Personal Loan #1	$2,000	5%	$1,500	$50

Step 2: Choose debt repayment method

There are two primary ways to pay down debt—Avalanche Method and Snowball Method. Below is a breakdown of each debt repayment strategy:

- **Avalanche Method**
  - The avalanche method focuses on paying off the debt with the highest interest rate first.
  - How it works:
    - List all of your debts from highest to lowest interest
    - Pay the monthly minimum payment on each debt
    - For the debt with the highest interest, pay the minimum + extra
    - Once the higher-interest debt is paid off, take that payment and add it to the minimum payment of the debt with the next highest interest rate
    - Continue this process until all debt is paid off

Here is an example:

Name of Lender	Principal Balance	Interest	Remaining Balance	Minimum Monthly Payment
Credit Card #1	$5,000	21.89%	$2,000	$45 + extra
Credit Card #3	$8,000	20.99%	$7,000	$210
Credit Card #2	$4,000	19.84%	$1,000	$40
Auto Loan #1	$25,000	6.63%	$20,000	$480
Student Loan #1	$80,000	6.625%	$69,000	$500
Personal Loan #1	$2,000	5%	$1,500	$50

The benefit of using the debt avalanche method is that you pay less total interest. As a result, you can get out of debt sooner and save more money in the long-run.

A disadvantage of using the debt avalanche method is that it may take longer to see progress because you are prioritizing paying off debt with the highest interest rate first, regardless of their balance. If your highest interest debt is also the debt with the highest balance, it may seem like your balance is not being paid down and that it is taking a long time. This can be discouraging.

- **Snowball Method**
  - The Snowball Method prioritizes paying down the debt with the lowest balance first.
  - How it works:
    - List all of your debts from lowest to highest balance
    - Pay the minimum monthly payment on each debt
    - For the debt with the lowest balance, pay the minimum + extra
    - Once the debt with the lowest balance is paid off, take that payment and add it to the minimum payment of the debt with the next lowest balance
    - Repeat this process until all debt is paid off

Here is an example:

Name of Lender	Principal Balance	Interest	Remaining Balance	Minimum Monthly Payment
Credit Card #2	$4,000	19.84%	$1,000	$40 + extra
Personal Loan #1	$2,000	5%	$1,500	$50
Credit Card #1	$5,000	21.89%	$2,000	$45
Credit Card #3	$8,000	20.99%	$7,000	$210
Auto Loan #1	$25,000	6.63%	$20,000	$480
Student Loan #1	$80,000	6.625%	$69,000	$500

The benefit of using the Snowball method is that you experience small wins early on in the process. These small wins can help you stay motivated to stick to your plan. A disadvantage of the Snowball Method is that it will cost you more money because you end up paying more interest overtime.

A third strategy involves a combination of both repayment methods. For instance, you may start with the Snowball Method because you want to pay down the smallest debt first in order to build momentum and confidence. This method offers a quick win compared to paying off a larger debt with high interest, which may take longer. Once you've paid the debt with the smallest balance, you may switch over to paying off the debt with the highest interest rate next. This third strategy is a balanced approach to paying down debt. Regardless of which method you choose, pick the method that fits your situation and is sustainable.

An important note I want to highlight—best case scenario is that you are able to pay the minimum monthly payment on each of your debts, plus paying extra on the highest interest debt or lowest balance. However, if you are unable to do this, focus on paying only the monthly minimums for each of your debts on-time for now. Paying the minimum monthly payments on-time can help you avoid late fees and credit score damage. With that being said, make a plan to contribute more money towards debt as soon as possible.

Step 3: Automate

Automating your bill payments works just as well as automating your savings! As mentioned previously, automate your bill payments to stay on-time and avoid late fees, as well as help improve your credit score. Improving your credit score is one of the best things you can do to improve your financial security net.

Paying off debt can be challenging, but it's not impossible. As you navigate the debt repayment process, consider some of these debt-slaying tips to make steady progress:

- **Avoid using your credit card**
  - As much as possible, avoid putting more debt onto your credit card by using your debit card or cash instead. Once you pay off a credit card, put it somewhere you can't easily access it.

- **Waive Late Fees**
  - Many credit card issuers may be willing to waive the late fee upon request, so shoot your shot and make that call.
  - If your initial request is declined, consider reaching out to the credit card company again after a few months of consistently paying your monthly credit card bills on time.

- **Lower APR on credit cards**
  - Request to have interest rates lowered on credit cards. Lowering the APR not only reduces the amount of interest paid over time, but it can also expedite the debt repayment process.
  - If your initial request for a lower APR is declined, don't be discouraged. Reach out to the credit card company again after a few months of consistently paying your monthly credit card bills on time. You cannot afford to leave anything on the table!

- **Pay more than once a month**
  - This can help you pay down the debt you are working on faster. The sooner you pay this debt down, the sooner you can rollover your payments to the next debt you want to tackle.

- **Calculate the number of payments left on debt**
  - Calculating the number of payments you have left on the debt you have chosen to attack first will give you an estimate on how long it will take you to pay down your debt. You can use an online calculator to get an exact number or you can estimate the number by using this formula:
    - Amount owed divided by the total payment you intend to make.
  - This estimate may be off a few months because it doesn't include interest; however, it is easy to estimate if you don't have access to an online calculator.

- **Consolidate debts**
  - There are debt consolidation companies that offer debt consolidation programs that allow you to combine multiple debts into a single monthly payment. The company then takes your payments and forwards them to all your creditors and lenders. This can be helpful because you don't have to make multiple payments every month. As for your interest rate, it may or may not be lowered. There are often fees associated with consolidating and you run the risk of having your credit score lowered. Debt consolidation does *NOT* eliminate your debt! Instead, it takes your exact debt load and moves it to a different place.
    - Before consolidating, it's a good idea to see if consolidation is right for you. If you would like assistance with consolidating your debt or have any questions, you can reach out to the following:
      - National Foundation for Credit Counseling
        www.nfcc.org
        (800) 388-2227
      - Financial Counseling Association of America
        www.fcaa.org

- **Put unexpected money towards your debt**
  - It will be tempting to spend that extra money on things that aren't essential needs. So pay yourself first by putting a huge portion of the lump sum towards debt and savings.

- **Sell items that you no longer need or use**
  - With the money you make, put it towards the debt you are working on. This may be tough to do in the beginning because you may not want to say goodbye to these items. If you're struggling to get rid of items, ask yourself "How does this serve my purpose?" By asking yourself this question, you are determining what value that item brings to your purpose. You can also use this method to realize that its purpose *is* helping you gain financial security.

- **Return items that you don't need**
  - If you purchased something you don't need and are still able to return it, return the item and put that returned money towards debt. Act as if that money was supposed to go towards debt to begin with.

- **Negotiate personal loans with 0% interest**
  - If you have a personal loan with a family member and/or friend and have a good relationship with them, see if you can negotiate monthly payments and payment timeline. Be honest and transparent about your situation. If you tell them that you will use the money to pay down other debts, make sure you pay down the other debts! Don't use that money to buy unnecessary things. Your family and friends trust that you will say what you do, so if you don't do what you say, you can break the trust you have with your family and friends. Your goal is to have open communication and a collaborative approach with them. Lastly, express gratitude. Showing your appreciation

and being honest goes a long way in maintaining a healthy relationship with them.

- **Continue to fund your emergency fund**
  - ○ By building your emergency fund, you can avoid putting unexpected debt on a credit card. Instead, you can pull money for future emergencies from your emergency fund.

There will be some months when you're able to pay extra and some months when you can't. Ultimately, the most important thing is that *you* find a system that works for *YOU* and keeps you motivated to pay down your debt!

Next Steps

Follow the checklist below to get started.

- ☐ **Download and review free copy of credit report from www.annualcreditreport.com**
  - ○ Verify name, address, Social Security number, date of birth, phone numbers, and employers
  - ○ Ensure all information is up-to-date and correct
  - ○ If you find incorrect information, reach out to the credit reporting company and file a dispute

If you suspect identity theft, report it at identitytheft.gov

- ☐ **Create debt repayment plan**
  - ○ List out all debt
  - ○ Choose strategy—Avalanche, Snowball, or both
  - ○ Automate bill payments

- ☐ **If you don't have credit, look into opening a secured credit card to start building credit**

11

DOCUMENT EVERYTHING

Building an emergency fund and improving your credit score requires time, so it is important that you remain committed to funding your emergency savings and reducing your debt over time. With all four corners of your financial safety net established, the best way to tighten each of them is to meticulously document *everything*. Not only do you want to gather all of your financial documents and keep them organized, you also want to document the abuse.

Documenting any incidents of abuse serve two main purposes:

1) **Building a Legal Case**
   In the event that you chose to take legal action or go to the police, this documentation would serve as evidence and could potentially strengthen your case. The more evidence you collect, the better.

2) **Creating a Record for Safety**
Having these incidents on record could ensure that there was tangible proof in case anything happens to you.

I know this sounds scary and you may be afraid to report any kind of domestic violence and/or abuse to the police. I want you to know that depending on what state you are in, there may be bills or laws in place that help individuals who have experienced financial abuse.

For example, in California, Senate Bill 975 "provides the opportunity to seek relief from debt repayment for coerced debt. It allows individuals to establish a debt was coerced by providing evidence including, but not limited to, a police report, FTC identity theft report, relevant court orders, and other documents provided by listed professionals."

In this situation, having these legal documents can strengthen an individual's case and can help them establish financial stability.

How to Document Abuse

Documenting abuse can help you with legal protection and your personal safety. Here are some effective ways to document these incidents:

- **Journal Entries**
  - Write in a journal documenting each incident in great detail. Include dates, times, places, and witnesses (if any).

- **Photographic Evidence**
  - Whenever possible, take photos of any physical injuries. Additionally, if possible, take pictures of surroundings post-incident.

- **Digital Evidence**
  - Screenshot any texts, emails, or social media posts that are threats or harassments. Include dates and times.

- **Recordings**
  - If it is legal in your state to record, you may be able to document threatening or harassing conversations using a recording device. Regulations vary from state to state, so if you are uncertain whether recording is admissible and legal, please seek legal advice. You could potentially get yourself into trouble if you record a conversation in a state that requires the other person to consent.
  - When it comes to recordings, there are two federal laws to be aware of. The "One-party consent law" allows you to record a phone call or in person conversation as long as you are a party to the conversation. If you are not a party to the conversation, you can record a conversation or phone call only if at least one party consents to the recording.

As of January 2022, the *"One-Party Consent"* States are:

Alabama	Louisiana	Rhode Island
Alaska	Maine	South Carolina
Arizona	Minnesota	South Dakota
Colorado	Missouri	Tennessee
District of Columbia	Nebraska	Texas
Georgia	New Jersey	Utah
Hawaii	New Mexico	Virginia
Idaho	New York	West Virginia
Indiana	North Carolina	Wisconsin
Iowa	North Dakota	Wyoming
Kansas	Ohio	
Kentucky	Oklahoma	

In situations where consent is required from ALL involved parties under some or all circumstances, this is known as the *"Two-Party Consent Law."* The states that uphold this law include:

California	Maryland	New Hampshire
Connecticut	Massachusetts	Oregon
Delaware	Michigan	Pennsylvania
Florida	Montana	Vermont
Illinois	Nevada	Washington

What to Do With Financial Documents and Abuse Documentation

Once you've gathered all this information, here are some effective ways to document your financial documents:

- **Gather relevant statements**
  - These include bank statements, investment statements, tax forms, invoices, receipts, bill statements, insurance policies, and any loan agreements.
  - If your name is on an account, such as a joint bank account, you are entitled to accessing those accounts and their statements.

- **Organize all documents**
  - Sort documents into categories that make it easy for you to find them. You can organize the documents into categories such as income, expenses, housing, taxes, insurance, photos, legal documents such as court orders, etc. At the end of the day, choose an organization method that works best for you.

- **Secure access**
  - Keep documents in a safe place that is inaccessible to your partner. If you are keeping things saved on a laptop or online, turn on password-protection. Consider creating a separate email account specifically for this documentation.

- **Make digital copies**
  - If you have any physical documents, consider scanning them so that you have a digital copy of each document. This can make it easier to store the documents on your laptop, in your email, and your online filing system.
  - Phone apps like Adobe Scan, Microsoft Lens, and CamScanner allow you to scan and convert physical documents into digital documents.

- **Backup files**
  - Backup all your digital files regularly. When you backup these files, add them to an external hard drive, cloud storage, and/or send them to a spare email. Having these documents in multiple places can help prevent this data from being lost.

Keep in mind that each state has distinct laws on how documentation can be used in court. If you are uncertain about what is permissible in your state, consider reaching out to The National Domestic Violence Hotline at (800) 799-7233 or www.womenslaw.org to find the contact information of a legal advocate in your area.

Next Steps

Follow the checklist below to get started.

- ☐ **Gather all financial documents and abuse documentation**
  - Bank statements
  - Investment statements

- Tax forms
- Invoices
- Receipts
- Bill statements
- Insurance policies
- Loan agreements
- Journal entries
- Witness statements (if any)
- Photographic and/or digital evidence of abuse

☐ **Sort and organize all documents**

☐ **Create separate email**

☐ **Upload and backup all documents**

12

H.E.L.P.

On November 20, 2016, I was in the kitchen preparing dinner after a heated argument with Feo. As I stood at the kitchen counter chopping tomatoes, I realized that I had forgotten the black pepper and fresh garlic. I walked over to the pantry and pulled the black pepper from the spice rack. I scanned the shelves for the garlic, but it wasn't in its usual place. Frustrated, I bent down and I began to search the lower shelf.

Feo stepped up behind me and asked, "Hey, can you give me a hand with this?" Given that we had just gotten into an argument, I retorted, "why don't you ask your bitch for help?"

In a split second, his temper flared. He picked up the knife from the chopping board and flung it at me. I quickly moved to the right, throwing myself onto the door of the pantry, barely dodging the knife. From the corner of my eye, I saw him pick up the tomatoes then throw them at me. In that heart-stopping moment, all I saw was black. Lights out. Nothing.

As I yelled at him, he grabbed me by the neck and slammed me against the wall. Fearful for my life, I struggled to fight back. I grabbed onto his arms, trying to pull his hands away from my neck, and I started kicking violently. A powerful kick to his knee forced him to release his grip.

My throat ached. Wheezing, I pushed past him and ran to the bedroom. He followed me and shoved me onto the bed, back first. Before I could get up, he got on top of me, wrapping his hands around my neck once more, strangling me. I laid on my back, kicking and screaming, "You're hurting me! You're hurting me!"

He ignored me.

It felt like forever before he let go of me. Breathing heavily and gasping for air, I rolled over and fell off the bed.

I quickly got up and I fled towards the front door. As I frantically looked for my bag, cell phone, and car keys in the living room, he eerily stood there watching me. In a calm voice, he asked "Are you leaving me?" as if nothing happened. I found my bag and ran out of the apartment, sprinting towards my car. I drove down the street and called a coworker, explaining the harrowing incident with tears running down my face. Without hesitation, she insisted I come over immediately. Forty-five minutes later, I found myself wrapped in her comforting embrace, tears streaming down my face.

"You are not going back to your place, Justine. It's not safe. You are staying here for the night," my friend declared firmly, pulling out an air mattress. "That's final."

The next morning, I woke up exhausted and confused. I was still trying to wrap my head around what happened the night before. After talking it out with my coworker, I knew the right thing for me to do was make the jump and leave my relationship. I had a long, difficult road ahead of me, but it was necessary for my safety. I was scared out of my mind, but I knew I had my emergency fund and financial safety net. I would be able to figure this out, someway somehow.

As I sat at my coworker's kitchen table, I called my childhood friend, Russ. For as long as I'd known Russ, he had always been a reliable anchor in my life. He cared deeply for his friends and family. Russ was also that person who happened to know everyone, or at least that's what it seemed like. His vast network of connections seemed to span all walks of life, a true testament to his ability to bring people together.

When his familiar voice greeted me, I felt this wave of relief wash over me. I began to share my traumatic experience from the night before. He replied, "Let me see what I can do."

I waited anxiously for him to call me back. When he did, it was with the news that a friend of his, Lyn, was willing to take me in while I figured things out. Tears of joy welled up and a waterfall of "thank you's" came pouring out of me.

After finishing work that day, I went home when I knew Feo was at work. I swiftly packed my bags, and headed to Lyn's place. Nervous and anxious during the drive, I also felt a comforting sense of hope. As I approached San Francisco, the bright lights of the Bay Bridge sparkled before me. It was as if those bright lights were a sign that there was light at the end of a very long dark tunnel.

I parked my car, clutching my bag tightly, and walked up to Lyn's door. Closing my eyes, I took a deep breath, exhaling slowly. I opened my eyes slowly then pressed the doorbell. Although it was likely only a few minutes of silence, the wait for the door to open felt like a lifetime. When it finally did, a huge, warm smile greeted me.

"Hi! Come in!" Lyn exclaimed.

I froze, staring at her. Why did she look familiar? Then it hit me. We had crossed paths a few years back. "We've met before, right?"

She chuckled, "Yeah, at *your* house party!"

We burst into laughter. Clearly, I had such a great time at that party that I forgot we had met. I stepped into her home and we spent the rest of the night catching up.

Although Lyn said I could stay as long as I wanted, I knew I needed to prioritize handling my situation back home. The following day I came up with a plan that I dubbed **H.E.L.P.**

Housing

Securing a new place to live, as soon as possible, became my top priority. During this time, I needed a place that was safe and financially accessible. In addition to the monthly rent, there were common expenses I kept in mind when looking for a place:

- Deposit, first and second month's rent
- Utilities (water, gas, electric, trash)
- Furniture and appliance costs
- Utility setup charges
- Security systems
- Moving costs
- Internet

After checking my savings fund and budget, I initially came up with this list:

- **Furnished**
  - I wanted a furnished apartment so that I wouldn't spend money on furniture.

- **Rent and utilities at $1000 or under**
  - This was the amount I was willing to pay for rent. If I could find a place cheaper, that would be the best case scenario.

- **Utilities included**
  - Having the utilities included in the rent could help me save money on additional move-in fees, such as activation and transfer fees. It would also save me time and energy from having to reach out to utility providers.

- **Studio or shared space**
  - Ideally, I wanted to have a place on my own. The cheapest option would have been a studio. If I couldn't find that, I was open to sharing a space with female-only roommates. At the time, I didn't feel comfortable living with men.

- **In a neighborhood far away from him**
  - I wanted to be close to my job, but as far away as possible from Feo. The last thing I wanted was to run into him.

When it came to looking for a place of my own, instead of going to a broker or speaking with a realtor, I scoured websites such as Craigslist. During my lunch breaks and after work, I drove around different neighborhoods looking for "for rent" signs. When I found one, I immediately called the number displayed. If there was no answer, I'd jot down the address and phone number, and try again later.

When I wasn't looking for places in person, I tirelessly submitted applications to one apartment listing after another. Some places didn't respond, and others had already secured tenants. This entire process left me exhausted.

At times, I felt like giving up. Yet, I remembered Justine who became resilient during her time in Istanbul amid civil unrest. I remembered Justine who fought back while being pinned on the bed. Then I remembered my *Why*.

I found just enough tenacity within me to persevere.

Thanksgiving was approaching, and I planned to celebrate it with my parents in Southern California. I eagerly anticipated reuniting with my parents. The weight of recent events hung heavy in the air, especially after telling them about the harrowing ordeal with Feo. They were very concerned about me and were looking forward to spending Thanksgiving weekend together.

I went back to my apartment the night before I left for Southern California. This wasn't the first time I had been back since the attack; I had slowly been picking up items I needed. Each time I crossed the threshold, memories of the attack would cross my mind. I made sure to come during the day while Feo was at work, so I could avoid interacting with him in person, despite having spoken to him via text and phone a few times. As I was packing my bags, Feo walked into the room; startling me. I glanced at him before hastily throwing the rest of my clothes into my suitcase.

"Where are you going? Am I invited?" he asked.

"No, you're not."

"You're going to leave me all alone?" Feo had the gall to sound hurt.

Confusion crossed my face, but I quickly reminded myself that I couldn't expect anything different from him. Such comments were sadly expected. Without saying a word, I zipped up my suitcase, turned around, and walked out of the apartment with my head held high.

The day after Thanksgiving, I was having dinner with my parents when my phone rang. Glancing at the screen, I recognized the number—it was a landlord I recently spoke to.

I politely excused myself from the table and walked outside. I nervously picked up the call, "Hello?"

"Hi, Justine! I'm calling to let you know that we are offering the place to you. When can you start the move-in process?" the man asked.

Stopping in my tracks, I burst into a million "thank you's" and began to cry tears of joy. It felt as though a tremendous weight had been lifted from my shoulders. I hurried back into my parents' home to share the great news. It seemed like everything was finally falling into place.

I ended up moving into a 100 sq ft. cottage that cost me $1,200 a month for rent. Although this was over my budget, after careful consideration, I was willing to pay the extra $200 since this place included utilities. It came furnished with a mini fridge, foldable futon, small table, one chair, and a freestanding clothes rack. The cottage itself was located in the backyard of the house where my landlord lived. It brought me comfort knowing that the landlord was close by. My place was located right next to a shopping plaza that had a pharmacy, grocery store, laundry mat, bank, restaurants, and stores. Across from the plaza was the subway station. The drive to work would be longer; however, I liked everything else about this place. I felt incredibly grateful.

Looking for a place takes time and patience. As you navigate the process of finding a place to rent, ask yourself these questions:

- Do I have enough money for the deposit, first and last months' rent?
- Do I know the essential features I need in my accommodations?
- Can I pay the rent without being late for a single payment?

- Am I close to markets, public transportation, pharmacies?
- Is there a landlord or property manager on-site?
- Do I feel safe in this neighborhood?
- Do I have proof of income?
- Do I have references?

In the end, renting a place involves expenses beyond just paying the monthly rent. How you have managed your money up until this point will make a difference on what kind of rental property you qualify for. So continue to fund your emergency fund and pay all bills on time, so when the time comes, you are ready.

Next Steps

Follow the checklist below to get started.

- ☐ **Consider the features and amenities you <u>need</u> (not want) for your lifestyle**
- ☐ **Review your budget**
- ☐ **Start researching locations and rental application process**
- ☐ **Continue to fund emergency fund and pay bills on time**

Embrace the capacity for zero

When I returned to the North Coast, I contacted my current landlord to explain the situation and requested the return of my $2,000 deposit. Despite his sympathy for my circumstances, he informed me he was unable to return the deposit as the lease was still active, and Feo was still living in the apartment. I tried negotiating by asking the landlord if he could return my $2,000 and ask Feo for $2,000, but he couldn't fulfill my request.

My reality struck me and struck me hard—I needed to come to terms with the fact that letting go of everything in my apartment was necessary. I needed to have the *capacity for zero* — the ability to start over and rebuild. While my heart yearned to keep fighting for what I believed I deserved, it would be smarter for me to conserve my energy and time. It was more sensible to redirect my efforts towards something that was guaranteed—my actions and attitude. I let go of any expectations I had of Feo returning the money to me after the lease ended. Although $2,000 could have made a significant difference in my situation, my life far outweighed the monetary value.

Beyond the $2,000, I also decided to leave everything behind, including the furniture, tv, and appliances. Despite having paid for everything, I had no attachment to these materialistic possessions. They had served their purpose and would no longer serve my future. In the end, the only things I would take with me were all financial documents, my clothes, toiletries, and cookware my mother gave me.

Deciding what items to keep can be tricky. As you navigate this process, ask yourself if the item you want to keep is useful, valuable, and essential.

- **Useful:** This is an item that serves a practical purpose or is easy to use in a specific context.

- **Valuable:** This is an item that holds significant worth. It could hold monetary value, emotional or sentimental worth, practicality, or rarity.

- **Essential:** This is an item that is necessary for your livelihood.

To help narrow down the items to bring with you, see if the item can fit all three descriptions. The most important description is that it is essential. Ask yourself, "Can I live without this?" If you need that item to support your livelihood, take it with you. For example, items such as medication, clothes, toiletries, laptop, identification documents, transit cards, prepaid cards, cash, important phone numbers, and legal documents are items worth keeping. You can keep all of these necessary items in a discreet, lightweight emergency bag. Store it in a place that is safe and hidden, but easily accessible for you. This bag can ensure a safe and quick escape.

Next Steps

Follow the checklist below to get started.

- ☐ **Gather all financial documents and other important documents**
  - ○ Birth certificate
  - ○ SSN card
  - ○ Passport
  - ○ Credit/debit cards
  - ○ Marriage certificate
  - ○ Custody documents
  - ○ Prescriptions
  - ○ Health insurance cards
  - ○ Bank statements
  - ○ Tax records
- ☐ **Decide what necessary items you will keep**
- ☐ **Decide what items you will leave behind**

☐   **Prepare emergency bag**

Legal Assistance

Before we go any further, let me share a story from my undergrad days. I spent three years working at a court-based self-help center where I assisted self-represented litigants in family and housing law matters like divorce, child custody, and evictions. In my role, I provided neutral assistance and legal options. I learned a lot about the divorce process from both the petitioner and defendant perspectives. The most significant lesson I learned during my time there was that anyone, regardless of their background, had access to legal help as long as they were willing to seek it. If you were willing to help yourself, there were people willing to help you. Little did I know that several years later, the roles would be switched and I would be the Petitioner in my own divorce.

Fast forward to my situation—I knew what the paperwork looked like and understood what the divorce timeline could entail in California. I also knew how expensive the process could be. Hiring a lawyer and going to court would be the most expensive. Another option would be going through mediation. A mediator is a neutral third-party that helps you and your spouse work out the details of the parts of the divorce that you and your spouse do not agree on.

Mediators do not make the decision for you, but rather they help you find the best solution for both parties. The mediation process costs less than hiring a lawyer and going to court; however, it can still be expensive for many. The cheapest option is to file for divorce yourself. When you file for divorce yourself, you are the one who prepares and files all the legal documents. There are no legal fees and the only fee you would pay would be the court filing fees, which vary by state. This was the divorce option I was most familiar with. In the end, I made the intentional decision to file for divorce on my own at one of the self-help centers.

If you are married and unable to afford a divorce attorney, seeking legal assistance at a self-help center is a viable option. The divorce process can be lengthy, and the self-help process is no exception. While these centers provide the legal documents to fill out, you can bring supporting documents to help expedite the process. Here is a checklist of documents and information to bring with you:

- **Date of marriage:** Legal date of when you were married

- **The address of your spouse:** This is important because this is where the paperwork will be served
  - If you don't happen to have the address of your spouse, you may be able to serve by publication. Ask the self-help center if this is a possible option in your city and state.

- **List of Separate Property:** These are assets or debts acquired *before* marriage
  - Your assets include:
    - Real Estate
    - Furniture, appliances
    - Vehicles, boats, trailers
    - Savings Accounts
    - Checking Accounts
    - Cash
    - Life Insurance
    - Investments (stocks, bonds, mutual funds, ETFs)

- Retirement Accounts (401k, 403b, Roth IRA/IRA)
- Pension
  - Your debts include:
    - Credit cards
    - Student Loans
    - Personal loans
    - Taxes

- **List of Community Property:** These are assets or debts acquired *during* marriage
  - Your assets include:
    - Real Estate
    - Furniture, appliances
    - Vehicles, boats, trailers
    - Savings Accounts
    - Checking Accounts
    - Cash
    - Life Insurance
    - Investments (stocks, bonds, mutual funds, ETFs)
    - Retirement Accounts (401k, 403b, Roth IRA/IRA)
    - Pension
  - Your debts include:
    - Credit cards
    - Student Loans
    - Personal loans
    - Taxes

While having this information when you visit the self-help center would be beneficial, it is not necessary. The center provides assistance in filling out these forms. If you do not have this information with you or you do not know it, you will likely have to take the legal paperwork home and fill it out then. Once you are done filling out the paperwork, you will need to bring it back and have the overseeing attorney review everything. As you can see, this process takes time and energy.

Try to be prepared with all documents. From there, next steps will be laid out for you, including a filing fee for the paperwork; however, if you cannot afford the filing fee, ask to fill out a fee waiver. Every state and self-help center is different when it comes to filing fees and processes, so keep that in mind.

In addition to self-help centers, there are law offices that offer free consultations. In my case, since I was dealing with immigration and divorce, I called both immigration and family law offices. Most of these consultations are between 10-15 minutes, so come prepared with your questions in order to make the best use of your time.

Not sure what to ask the lawyers? Here are some questions you can ask the lawyer about the divorce process:

- What does the divorce process look like?
- How will we communicate throughout the process?
- What is community vs. separate property in my case?
- What would spousal support look like?
- What are the grounds for divorce in this state?
- What would child support and legal custody look like?
- Who is in charge of paying what debts?
- What steps do I need to take if domestic violence is an issue?
- How does domestic violence affect the divorce proceedings?

- How can we keep my personal information confidential due to safety concerns?

When it comes to the costs of hiring a lawyer, here are questions you can ask the lawyer:

- How much is your retainer?
- How much is your billable hourly rate?
- Do you offer payment plans or other financing options?
- Are you the only lawyer who is going to be billing against the retainer?
- How much are the hourly rates for everyone that will be working on my case?

Asking these questions can help you save money because you'll know how much is going to be billed against what and it can give you clarity on what the divorce process may entail.

At the end of the day, even if you are not thinking about getting a divorce, I still highly encourage you to speak with a lawyer and/or visit a self-help legal center to see what your options are. The more you know about the divorce process, the better you will be prepared to make an informed decision.

In addition to the self-help legal centers, there are Family Justice Centers that can assist. These are multi-agency, multi-disciplinary service centers that provide a variety of services to victims of domestic violence, intimate partner violence, sexual assault, child abuse, elder abuse, and human trafficking. At these centers, you can receive help with restraining orders, court preparation, housing, medical, and safety planning.

If you are currently feeling overwhelmed, scared, anxious, or confused, I want to take a moment and validate those feelings of yours. It is okay to feel this way. It is okay to not know what any of this means. It's normal, even. That's why we are going over it together.

Now before you go into a dark hole of negative self-talk, I want you to say this out loud, *"I am brave. What I am doing is not easy, but it is the right thing to do."*

The fact that you've picked up this book and read this far speaks volumes about who you are at this moment. Keep going!

Next Steps

Follow the checklist below to get started.

- ☐ **Speak with a lawyer to see what option works best for your situation**

- ☐ **Gather all information needed for divorce process**
  - ○ List of assets (separate and community property)
  - ○ List of liabilities (separate and community property)
  - ○ Personal information
  - ○ Financial documents
  - ○ Legal documents

To find the closest self-help center or Family Justice Center in your area, visit www.justinedeperalta.com. I have a dedicated Resources section to assist you.

Play chess

Leaving an abusive relationship is never easy and it isn't always the safest option. Statistics show that approximately seventy-five percent of women who are killed by their abusers are murdered when they attempt to leave or after they have left. According to the National Domestic Violence Hotline, "survivors of abuse return to their abusive partners an average of seven times before they leave for good."

This may sound unbelievable or unreasonable to someone who has never experienced abuse, but as we know, domestic violence is incredibly complex. There are several reasons why a person might stay or return to their abusive partner. I stayed because:

- I was embarrassed and ashamed that I had done something wrong.
- I accepted his poor behavior towards me as normal.
- I was initially afraid of the legal system.
- I wanted to try to make things work.
- I wanted to see if he would change.
- I was intimidated by his threats.
- I had incredibly low self-esteem.
- I felt incredibly sad and alone.

For all the times I went back to Feo and gave him another chance, I lost a small part of myself. But do you want to know what gave me the confidence to stop playing checkers and start playing chess?

It was the culmination of all the planning I had done over the past two years. You see, all the small, consistent steps I had taken were a representation of control I had for the very first time in a long time. I was in control of:

- Understanding where my money was going.
- Setting up and funding my emergency fund.
- Paying my debt payments on time.
- Managing my cash flow.
- Documenting the abuse.

I had the tools, knowledge, and confidence to start taking giant leaps. I was ready to jump ship...and jump *high*.

In the past, making short-term decisions led to long-term consequences so instead of fighting back with violence, having a poor attitude, and a victim mindset, I played the long-game. Aware of Feo's short temper, I found myself in a situation where I had to maintain the façade that everything was okay between us. I needed to make sure not to do anything that would upset or anger him. More importantly, I had to have absolute control of my attitude and actions towards him. I recognized that I couldn't control how he would behave with me, so I needed to focus on how I would behave with him.

Now, you should know that what I did next is not something I recommend doing. It was extremely dangerous. But I want to be fully transparent with you on how I was able to get Feo to agree to and sign a Joint Petition for Summary Dissolution. In California, a Joint Petition for Summary Dissolution allows you and your spouse to end a marriage without a trial. It's less expensive than the standard divorce process and there is less paperwork. However, there are certain requirements that need to be met. In general, this process is only for couples who:

- Have been married less than 5 years.
- Have lived in the state and county for a certain amount of time.
- Have no children together and cannot be pregnant.
- Own relatively little.

- Do not owe more than a certain amount of debt.
- Do not want spousal support.
- Agree on how to split any property.

All of these must be true in order to proceed with this process.

Before ever hearing about this option, I wanted Feo to go with me to the self-help legal center to file for standard divorce. This was the hardest part because I needed to strategically navigate my interactions with him. We were no longer living together, but I would pick up his phone calls and listen to him tell me about his day. I once met him for dinner at a restaurant. I wanted him to believe that we were "*okay.*" Even in a moment of weakness, I went back to the old apartment to talk things out. I asked him if he was willing to go to therapy and he refused. I asked him for a divorce and he refused. I am aware now that this was an incredibly dangerous situation I put myself in, but at the time, I needed to know that I tried everything I could.

One day, I looked up self-help legal centers around the North Coast. There were several centers in the vicinity. I strategically chose one close to the apartment that I used to share with Feo because I wanted to spend less time in the car with him since I would be driving us there. I didn't trust him to meet me there on his own. After two and half months of strategically playing nice, Feo agreed to go with me to the self-help center. On the drive to the self-help center, Feo went back and forth with his attitude towards me. One minute he would make fun of me and tell me I was too weak and stupid to file for divorce, then he would try to guilt trip me by saying that I was abandoning him.

I simply responded, "I'm just tired."

Once we got there, his entire mood shifted. He started getting annoyed and anxious. I think it started to set in that we were actually filing for divorce. After an hour of waiting, which felt like a lifetime, we were finally able to sit down with one of the overseeing attorneys. As we explained our situation to the attorney, he looked at us and said, "Have you thought about a Joint Petition for Summary Dissolution? You qualify."

My heart started to beat quickly. I looked at Feo and asked him if he would be willing to sign. He stared down at the document. Right before he stepped away from the table, the attorney told us that he could give us a few minutes to talk it out or, if we wanted, we could take the documents home, then bring the signed documents back another time. My hands became cold and clammy while my heart continued to beat quickly. Feo and I sat there in silence.

Eventually, I asked him again if he would be willing to sign. After thinking long and hard, Feo signed and dated the paperwork. I grabbed the documents and held on tightly to them. As we walked towards the exit, Feo started to yell at me in front of everyone. We ended up not filing the paperwork that day; and on the drive home he laughed and said, *"you're too stupid to file."*

Weeks had gone by and on the morning of February 28, 2017, I drank my coffee, showered, and got dressed. I threw my bag over my shoulder and headed out. As I drove south on the freeway, I passed my normal exit for work. I wasn't going to work that day. Instead, I was on my way to the courthouse to file the divorce papers.

I pulled into the courthouse parking lot and switched off the engine. I sat in my car, closed my eyes, and took a few deep breaths. "You got this, Justine," I whispered to myself. "You're going to be okay. You have the *capacity for zero*. The next chapter of your life starts *today*."

I wiped the tears from my eyes and got out of the car. I adjusted my blouse, pulled my shoulders back, and held my head high as I walked towards the courthouse. After passing through security, I asked where the filing window was and was directed down the hall. There were a few people standing in line when I got there. I anxiously waited in line until the clerk called me to the window. I handed her my paperwork, and nervously waited as she flipped through the documents, her expression unreadable.

"That'll be $435" she said. I handed her my credit card. As she processed the payment, I held my breath, hoping for a smooth transaction. When she was done, she handed back my credit card. "If everything goes through, your divorce will be finalized in six months. Have a good day."

I smiled back with tears in my eyes. I looked at her and responded, "Thank you. This is the best $435 I've ever spent." When I got back to my car, my emotions overwhelmed me. Tears of joy rolled down my face. I felt relief, gratitude, and newfound freedom.

Later that evening, Feo video called me to tell me about his day. I stared at him and when he was finally done talking, I took a deep breath and looked him in the eye.

"I filed for divorce today."

His face turned white and his smile disappeared. "Seriously?" he asked in disbelief.

"Yes," I confidently held his gaze, unwavering.

He hung up on me. I stared at a blank phone screen. That would be the last time I would ever see Feo.

Now is the time to be strategic more than ever. Thinking ahead strategically and intentional planning can equip you with the tools needed to effectively navigate the process of leaving. This includes assessing the situation, gathering all important documents, finding a support system, seeking professional help, and creating a safety plan. The more prepared you are, the more confident you become in making decisions that support your overall safety and wellbeing.

Next Steps

Follow the checklist below to get started.

- ☐ **Assess the situation**
- ☐ **Gather all important documents**
- ☐ **Set up a support system with trusted family and friends**
- ☐ **Seek professional help**

| Phase 3 |

THE LIGHT

13

RECOVER, HEAL, THRIVE

Jumping from high ground and landing on a net takes courage, but you did it! And this wasn't just any ordinary net. It was a net that *you* built. I'm so proud of you. As you lay in the middle of the net, you have two options:

A) You can lay in your net for a while, but the longer you stay there, you start to notice that it's getting a bit uncomfortable and restrictive.

B) You decide to crawl out of the net. It's not easy. Your foot may slip or you might fall over because of how shaky the net can be, but if you continue to crawl towards the edge, you can see freedom on the other side.

The crawl to the edge of your financial safety net is an example of what your recovery and healing journey is like after chaos. It's a journey marked by uncertainty, where progress can feel bumpy and shaky at times. Honestly, the path forward may seem daunting. Losing a relationship is hard and there is grief that comes with it. Afterall, you created a life with this person. Grief is a natural response to loss. It is also very complex. On some days, you'll feel sad and angry. On other days, you may feel confused and lonely. These emotions come and go with different intensities and vary from person to person.

However, days of happiness do exist! Grief can pave the way for new beginnings and opportunities of growth in different areas of our lives. In this chapter, we will learn ways to find happiness in our health, wealth, and relationships. If every move you make is driven with intentional decisions accompanied with deliberate practice, you position yourself for meaningful progress.

Remember this—you can build an empire after chaos.

Now is the time to build the life you deserve. One day at a time.

Everyone's recovery and healing journey will look and be different. In this chapter, I present the nine lifestyle changes I made to optimize my health, wealth, and overall well-being. Take what you want, then implement it in a way that best suits your journey.

Have difficult but honest conversations with yourself

When you lie to yourself, your ability to make decisions becomes clouded. However, when you embrace honesty and start being honest with yourself, you pave the way for better decision-making. By confronting your current reality, you're no longer doing what's easy, you're doing what's right for your personal growth.

The first step towards recovery begins with having honest conversations with yourself. I knew that if I wanted my situation to change and make space for personal growth, I would need to be honest with myself first. The first real question I asked myself was "Would you be in a relationship with yourself right now?" At first, I said "Yes! Why not?!" but then I realized I was rationalizing behavior that I knew deep down didn't align with my beliefs. I was:

- Not exercising even though I felt better when I did.
- Smoking cigarettes even though I felt terrible afterward.
- Spending money on drinking even though I disliked being hungover.
- Hanging out with people who negatively impacted me even though I didn't like them.
- Buying items with no long-term purpose even though they made me happy at the moment.

My *"come to Jesus"* moment happened one morning as I sat in front of my cottage with my usual menthol cigarette and black coffee. As I exhaled, I expected the taste of menthol to leave my body, but this time I didn't. Instead, I tasted burnt newspaper. Repulsed and confused, I took in another drag. Again—burnt newspaper. As someone who smoked a pack of cigarettes a day for several years, you'd think the taste of burnt newspaper wouldn't be out of the ordinary. But this time was different. I looked down at the cigarette and asked myself, "Why am I doing this? I don't even like you. You will be my last one. Ever."

Smoking had become muscle memory, a bad habit that I automated. It was also a habit that no longer aligned with my dreams and goals of becoming a healthier version of myself. After finishing my last inhale, I let out a big exhale as if I were getting rid of the old Justine. I took the pack of cigarettes and threw them into the large trash bin.

I walked into my cottage and grabbed my notebook and pen. After working through my defensiveness, I sat down and began to ask myself these questions:

- What is confusing/overwhelming/scary to me right now?
- Are you being heard or understood right now?
- Are you happy with your life right now?
- What is important to you right now?
- How are you feeling right now?
- What brings you joy now?

In these conversations with myself, I added the word *now* at the end of each question. Why? It kept me focused on the present. It refrained me from going into the past where I could easily wallow in regret and going into the future where I could create imagined troubles.

By being honest with yourself, a shift begins to happen:

- You begin to learn more about yourself and what you need.
- You create a reality that aligns with who you are.
- You uncover flaws that are holding you back.

Your very first honest conversation with yourself is the most important but also the *most difficult* because it will be the first time dissecting your feelings, needs, and thoughts after chaos.

As you prepare for these conversations with yourself, here is what you can do to set yourself up for success:

- **Pick a time and place**
  - The best conversations happen when you plan them, instead of spontaneously having them.

If possible, pick a time and place where it'll be quiet with little to no distractions.

- **Shut out all distractions**
  - Turn off your cell phone, mute all notifications, shut the door, and wear ear plugs.

- **Record everything**
  - Whether you type your conversations on your laptop or write them in a journal, have something with you to record the conversations. It may be helpful to revisit these conversations and see how far you've come.

- **Begin with a positive affirmation**
  - Having a positive affirmation to keep you grounded is going to be very important in combating any negative belief that comes your way during an honest conversation. I would say...
    - "You are deserving."
    - "You are worthy."
    - "You have the capacity for zero."
    - "You are given another opportunity to start over today."
    - "You are given another opportunity to be a better version of you today."

On the day of your honest conversation with yourself, the best thing you want to do for yourself is to give yourself grace. Be kind to yourself by practicing compassion with the old you. By following Marshall Rosenberg's communication strategy, Nonviolent Communication (NVC), you learn to communicate with empathy by focusing on expressing yourself with honesty and clarity.

- **Identify what you see and/or hear that bothers you**
  - This is not about what you think. It is what you actually observe that bothers you. For me, seeing my puffy red eyes from crying bothered me.

- **Identify your feelings tied to your observation**
  - Remember to identify the feeling you have, not your opinion. "I feel sad, overwhelmed, confused, angry..." When you use "I" statements, you put importance towards your feelings and you give them the power that they deserve.

- **Identify your needs**
  - Your needs "I feel angry because I need safety/security. I feel confused because I need guidance since I don't know where to start."

- **Make a clear, positive action request**
  - Make a list of all the things you are willing and not willing to do. As you navigate different topics, ask yourself "Am I willing to _____?" Once you have a list of all the things you are willing to do, your decision making becomes more clear and intentional.

By having these honest conversations with yourself, you identify your needs and validate your feelings. This creates a space for you to acknowledge what you are willing and not willing to do. Knowing what you are willing to do can help you say *no* to the things that do not serve your personal development.

Visualize who you want to become

When I was a little girl, my dad used to tell me to write my goals on a piece of paper and tape it to the ceiling above my bed. That way, every morning when I opened my eyes, my goals would be the first thing I saw. At the time, I didn't realize I was practicing *visualization*.

Visualizing who you want to become can be a powerful exercise in personal growth and self-discovery. It can increase your confidence and self-belief in what you want to succeed in. By picturing yourself achieving specific goals and milestones, you create a vision that guides you.

A great way to visualize who you want to become is by creating a vision board. A vision board is a collage of images, pictures, and affirmations of one's dreams and goals. It is designed to serve as a source of inspiration and motivation. A vision board should include a theme and/or goals that you are working towards. The images and words you put on your vision board depict what it is that you exactly want. To create your own vision board, start by asking yourself these questions:

- What areas of my life do I want to focus on?
- What values and beliefs are important to me?
- What emotions do I want to evoke when I look at my vision board?
- What specific goals or outcomes do I want to achieve in each of these areas?
- What obstacles do I anticipate on my journey and how do I plan on tackling them?

- Where will I display my vision board?

Answering these questions before creating your vision board can help you clarify your goals and stay focused on them.

Once you've set your vision board up, put it somewhere that allows you to see it every day. This could be the bathroom mirror, background of laptop or phone, or work desk. Spend a few minutes every day looking at your vision as a reminder to take action. Create a to-do list to help you turn your vision into reality.

Speak positively about yourself

For the first three months after moving to my new place, I would cry myself to sleep and wake up crying almost every day. One evening, I called Kali. As I spoke with her, I began to sob as I angrily spoke about Feo. Then I started turning on myself by saying "I'm so stupid. Why did I let this happen? How did I get myself into this?" As I continued my self-deprecating rant, she stopped me and said four words that would forever change my life: "Be kind to yourself."

I stopped talking. I was speechless. No one had ever said those exact words to me before. After a moment of silence, I wiped the tears off my face and replied, "You're right. I do need to be kind to myself." It was then that I truly realized how important self-talk was. For years, I had negatively beat myself up with my own words, on top of the psychological abuse from Feo. I went to bed that night with that thought laying heavily on my mind.

The morning after, I sat down with my coffee and I decided to make a list of three positive things I could say about myself:

- I'm funny

- I'm smart
- I'm compassionate

The next morning, I added three more positive things about myself to this list:

- I'm strong
- I'm willing to try
- I'm family-oriented

I continued to do this every morning for thirty days. I called this my "3 for 30" strategy. After thirty days, it became a habit to list three positive things about myself. As time went by, I added to this list anytime I thought of something kind to say to myself. If at any point I found myself speaking negatively about myself, I gently reminded myself that how I spoke to myself was a reflection of who I believed I was. In addition, I turned negative statements about myself into positive statements. For example, instead of saying "I can't," I said "I can." This perspective helped me have a more optimistic mindset overall.

How we talk to ourselves greatly impacts our decisions. Our decisions, then, influence our actions. Speaking positively about yourself ultimately helps you build confidence, self-esteem, and self-compassion needed for yourself and the relationships in your life. It contributes to your overall emotional well-being and happiness.

Seek professional help

My friends were absolute rock stars throughout, and I knew that they would be there with emotional support; however, they were not my therapists. A dramatic mindset shift was separating friends and therapy. At the end of the day, there is only so much that you can share with your friends before it becomes toxic and traumatic for everyone. In order to preserve my friendships, I decided to seek professional help.

Making this mindset shift and admitting that I needed to see a therapist was a huge decision, especially in my culture. In general, Filipinos are reluctant about formal help-seeking. For some, it's a sign of weakness or that you are crazy. As a result, they prefer to seek help from close family and friends. I knew I wasn't crazy and I knew that I needed help.

Starting therapy can feel daunting at first, but it is one of the bravest and most rewarding steps you can take on your healing journey. Remember that asking for help is not a sign of weakness. It is a form of strength. It is a decision that reflects your desire for a better life, and your willingness to take proactive steps to achieve it. Therapy is an investment in yourself and your future. There are many benefits to speaking with a therapist:

- Gives you an objective point of view of your situation
- Learn how to communicate feelings and needs
- Develop self-confidence and self-worth
- Explore thoughts, feelings, and needs
- Identify harmful patterns of behavior
- Learn techniques to manage stress
- Develop coping strategies

In addition to speaking with a therapist, it can be helpful to seek financial help from a financial coach, Certified Financial Planner (CFP), and/or Certified Financial Therapist (CFT-I). A CFP can advise clients on financial topics such as retirement, investments, tax planning, goal setting, and risk management. A financial therapist is a certified professional who provides therapy services with the goal of changing the way you think, feel, and behave about money. Their goal is to help clients explore their relationship with money, uncover root causes of financial trauma, and change their relationship with money.

As you start researching and looking for professional help, consider the following:

- If you have health insurance, see if therapy is covered.
- Ask how much the copay is.
- Do you need a referral?
- Is there a deductible that you need to meet before therapy sessions are covered?
- What kind of support would you like? In-person? Telehealth?
- What other supports/resources do they offer outside of 1:1 sessions?
- What are your goals and what do you hope to achieve through therapy?
- Make a list of all the qualities you want in a therapist.
- Research therapists and consider their qualifications, experiences, and therapeutic approaches.
- Are they easy to access (i.e. close to home, can walk, etc.)?

If you have a bad experience with a therapist, look for another. I certainly did. I attended two sessions with my first therapist before making the decision to stop seeing her. I didn't feel safe nor connected with her style of therapy. I continued my search and eventually found a therapist that I connected with almost immediately. The ability to say no to a therapist that doesn't serve you and yes to one that does is empowering and a confidence boost. So when I tell you that you don't have to stay with someone, I mean it. Use this opportunity to choose who you want to be with on your healing journey. You are going to be spending time with this person and sharing very personal details about your life, so choosing someone who fits your needs and who you feel comfortable with are important factors to consider.

Prioritize your health

The decision to quit smoking caused a domino effect. I decided to cut out or reduce anything that negatively affected my health with this three-step process:

- **List out all bad habits**
  - If it didn't align with my financial, health, and relationship goals, it was on this list.

- **Avoid temptation**
  - If something, someone, or someplace would tempt me to fall back into a bad habit, I avoided it altogether.

- **"Tomorrow" method**
  - If I found myself in a situation where I couldn't avoid temptation or I was having a moment of weakness, I used my "tomorrow" method. What is my "tomorrow" method? It is a strategy I use to procrastinate my bad habits. When I'm tempted to do something I shouldn't do, such as smoking, I would tell myself "tomorrow." When tomorrow came and I had another craving for a cigarette, I told myself "tomorrow." I repeated this process until I stopped having my cravings. This is the

one time procrastination worked in my favor because it put off something that didn't serve me anymore.

Following this process made my spending habits more intentional. The money that would have gone to drinking, partying, and eating out was spent on activities that helped with the improvement of my well-being: therapy, building my emergency fund, paying down debt, gym membership, yoga, healthier foods, hiking, and other activities.

One activity that I poured myself into and brought me so much joy was ice skating. I grew up a competitive figure skater and although I stopped competing when I was a teenager, I would go skating every now and then as an adult. However, I stopped doing it because I did not make it a priority anymore.

As I began to reinvent myself, I decided to start skating again. I called up the local ice rink and asked them how much a public session would cost or freestyle session. Once I figured out the numbers, I looked at my budget and made adjustments so that I could afford going ice-skating. When my skate touched the ice for the very first time after ten years, it felt like I had never stopped. I skated a few laps and I began to cry, falling in love with skating all over again. I started skating every weekday morning, doing the 4 AM freestyle session for an hour. Once my skating session was done, I drove back to my place, showered, ate, and got ready for the workday.

Being back on the ice really helped my mental health; and it made me realize that prioritizing my mental health was the most important during this time. Since I was prioritizing my mental health, I was intentional with my budget and I wanted to make sure that I had the money to support this activity because I knew in the long run this would help my overall well-being.

The best gift you can give yourself is your health. Your health allows you to do the things you love with the people you love. We can lose ourselves when we are in survival mode. You spend time doing the things that don't serve your overall well-being. Now is the time for you to start doing the things that bring you joy.

If you're unsure of what to work on first, start with small improvements to your daily activities: Incorporate twenty minutes of movement, drink at least eight 8oz glasses of water with electrolytes, avoid using bluescreens one hour before bed, avoid looking at your phone first thing in the morning, eat whole unprocessed foods, aim for at least seven hours of sleep, spend time outdoors, and surround yourself with positive people. Applying these changes to your daily life can help you build healthier habits and live the fulfilling life you deserve.

Surround yourself with positive and encouraging people

I'm going to hit you with a hard truth—not everyone is going to be compassionate or understanding to your story. There will be people who pretend they care, but are secretly happy to see you fail. There are those who are nice to your face, but talk badly behind your back. So remember this—you are not for everyone and not everyone is for you.

While I knew that my recovery ultimately came down to me, I became very selective on who I shared my story with and who I surrounded myself with. I intentionally surrounded myself with positive, supportive friends that I could trust. These are people I could be completely raw and vulnerable with, especially on days that seemed more difficult. As I poured my heart out to them, they not once judged me or told me what to do. They created a safe space for me to talk, as they listened and supported my decisions.

One way I made time and created space for my friends was by going on trips with them and creating experiences. Whether it was me flying to Germany or Seattle, or going to a local winery or ice cream shop, I loved spending time with the closest women in my life. It brought me joy and comfort being surrounded by women who loved me unconditionally.

As you think about who you want to surround yourself with, consider the following:

- They are not judgmental.
- They don't tell you what to do.
- They remain open and supportive.
- They listen and support your decisions.
- They encourage small steps and provide options.
- They don't pressure you to take drastic measures.

Surrounding yourself with positive, supportive people contributes to your overall well-being and can have a profound impact on your mindset and mood. They can motivate and inspire you to become the best version of yourself *because* they give you that space to grow.

On the other end, surrounding yourself with negative people can take you away from your journey to healing. Negative people can drain your energy and bring you down. Have you ever heard of the *crab mentality*? Imagine a bucket of crabs. When one of them tries to climb out, another crab grabs onto the one climbing out, preventing them from trying to leave. This is what happens to you when you surround yourself with negative people.

If you're looking to build a community that is aligned with your goals and needs, you can start by putting yourself in environments with like-minded individuals. Chinese philosopher Confucius once said, "If you are the smartest person in the room, then you are in the wrong room." Attend workshops, conferences, and events where the attendees either share the same vision as you or possess the qualities you strive to have. This will challenge you to step out of your comfort zone and help you become a better version of yourself.

In the end, do your best to protect your peace by surrounding yourself with people who encourage you to be a better version of you. These are people who cheer you on as you go through a rollercoaster of emotions. They don't judge you and they accept who you are and who you are becoming.

Spend time alone

Nothing helped me learn more about myself than the days that I intentionally spent by myself in nature. Research from Cornell University states that as little as ten minutes in nature left individuals feeling happier and less stressed. As part of my healing journey, I created "Solitude Sundays" or "Silent Sundays." On Sundays, I would disconnect from society and would spend the day in nature. I'd pick different hikes in the area and I would do a new hike every Sunday. In order for me to be fully present, I muted notifications on my cell phone, didn't pick up phone calls or respond to text messages. By allowing myself to disconnect from the world, I made space to rediscover and reconnect with myself for the first time in years.

There are several benefits to spending time with yourself. When you are alone, you have the opportunity to:

- Self-reflect
- Be creative
- Reduce stress
- Build self-reliance

- Increase self-esteem
- Practice mindfulness
- Enjoy nature's healing
- Understand your feelings

The more you spend time alone, the more you cultivate a deeper understanding of yourself. You know what you like and don't like. You gain clarity and confidence to make decisions that lead to a more fulfilling life. The time I spent alone helped me build a strong sense of self. I became so comfortable with my own company that I didn't need to fill space just to fill space. I became more intentional with who I spent my time and energy with. I went from spending time with people to fill a void to spending time with people I cared about and genuinely wanted in my life.

The longest relationship you'll ever be in is with yourself. Make it the relationship you deserve!

Congratulate yourself for every win

For the first two months after filing for divorce, I hadn't blocked Feo from my phone, emails, and social media. He called and emailed me every single day, but I ignored him. I wasn't talking to him anymore, and figured he'd eventually stop reaching out to me. One day he called me and I reluctantly picked up. "I just called to tell you that I met someone new," he said. "I wouldn't expect anything more from you. Anything else?" I calmly responded then hung up. Without skipping a beat, I blocked him from my phone, email, and social media. At that very moment, I cut the second to last string tying me to Feo.

It felt so damn good.

When you've been in survival mode for so long, it is a lot easier to accept failure. As a result, we may find ourselves forgetting what progress looks like. As you begin to heal, one of the ways you can regain control of your life is by creating a space that is comforting and celebratory. Officially blocking Feo from all forms of communication was a big win for me. I learned how to congratulate myself for every win I had— whether big or small. Two of my favorite ways I'd celebrate myself would be buying myself flowers and getting massages. How you celebrate yourself is up to you. It could be:

- A pat on the back
- Watching a movie
- A compliment to yourself
- Going for a leisurely walk
- Write a kind letter to yourself
- Buy yourself fresh cut flowers
- Treating yourself to a massage
- Surrounding yourself with loved ones
- Going out to dinner and ordering your favorite dish

Celebrating small wins is just as important as celebrating big wins. Small wins can release dopamine, a hormone and neurotransmitter that can improve your mood and motivation. By celebrating your small wins, you build more confidence to achieve the bigger goals you have set for yourself.

Don't compare yourself to others

Theodore Roosevelt once said, "comparison is the thief of joy." And he's right. Comparing yourself to others can lead to negative self-talk and low self esteem. You may struggle finding happiness with what you have because you are focused on what you don't have when comparing yourself to others.

As you begin to gain confidence, you may be inclined to share your wins with others. You will meet others who are in the same space with you, who want to tell you their relationship problems. When you compare yourself with them, you rob yourself of *your truth*. At the end of the day, it is not a competition as to who suffered the most. It is about building community with compassion.

If you find yourself negatively comparing yourself to others, start by practicing gratitude. Shift your focus to what you currently have and what you've experienced. Spend a few minutes daily listing out three things you are grateful for and how they have positively impacted your life. Remember this—no one in this world has ever lived a second of your life. So put your blinders on and continue to do you, boo!

Your healing journey is exactly that—a journey. It's not just about the outcomes. You'll experience highs, lows, and everything in between. Be patient, have fun, and enjoy your adventure!

Conclusion

After living in my cottage for seven months, it was time to move back to Southern California and start the next chapter of my life. I moved in with my parents with the intention of moving out once I settled into my new job.

As the date approached for when my divorce would be finalized, I began to check my P.O. Box almost every day. In late August 2017, I drove to the post office and opened my mailbox. In front of me was an envelope staring back at me. I took a deep breath and slowly opened the envelope. I pulled the piece of paper out and began to unfold it. My eyes scanned the top, "Judgment of Dissolution and Notice of Entry of Judgment." I began to read the next line. "A judgment of dissolution of marriage will be entered, and the parties are restored to the status of single persons, effective..." I began to cry tears of joy.

The final string tying me to Feo was officially cut.

I was finally free.

In early November 2018, I excitedly walked into Bob's furniture store, shopping for my new home. As I entered the store, a friendly woman greeted me with a big, warm smile. "Is there something you're looking for in particular?"

"Furniture. Brand new furniture," I responded back with an equally big smile on my face.

She nodded. "Is there a specific piece of furniture you want to look at?"

"All of it. I want to look at all of it," I goofily replied, looking around the showroom floor. "I'll take a look around and let you know if I have any questions."

Making a beeline for the bed section, I touched every piece of furniture enroute. As I walked around the bed section, I gently touched each and every one of them. I took my time as I laid in each of the beds I was interested in. As I laid on one of the beds, a sales rep approached me and asked me what my thoughts were on the bed. Gazing up at the ceiling, I couldn't help but smile. "It's exactly how I like my bed—firm enough to provide support, but soft enough for me to feel safe. I'll take it."

With the bed checked off my list, it was time for me to look at the couches. As I wandered around the store looking at the different options, I wanted my vision to come to life. I was determined to infuse color into my new home. Red, orange, green, yellow...I wanted all of it. I had lived in darkness for so long that it was now time for me to bring COLOR into my life.

As I sat on an emerald green velvet couch, the woman who greeted me earlier approached me again to see if I needed anything.

"I *love* the color of this couch," I told her, touching the couch I was sitting on.

"I think it's beautiful. It matches your personality," she kindly responded. Had she been watching me this whole time as I happily walked around the store? I looked up at her and began to cry. Confused, she asked, "Oh no! Are you okay?"

"I'm just so happy," I wiped tears from my face. "For the first time in my life, I'm not asking a partner for their opinion.

I'm not buying a used couch. No one is financially helping me. Everything I buy today will be mine."

Tears began to form in the woman's eyes and she reached out her arms and asked if she could hug me. So there I was, standing in the middle of Bob's furniture, crying tears of happiness in the arms of a total stranger.

I will never forget how empowered I felt that day. Every decision and action I made over the past 3 years led to this moment—I was in control of my life and happiness. All because I decided to build my own financial safety net and trusted myself enough to jump. After reading this book, now *you* can build your *own* financial safety net and reclaim the freedom you rightfully deserve!

Glossary

Annual Percentage Rate (APR): The annual rate of interest charged to borrowers by lenders.

Annual Percentage Yield (APY): The annual rate of return on an investment.

Asset: Something physical or intangible that contains economic value and/or future benefit.

Automatic transfer: A banking arrangement where funds are moved between accounts on a regular basis without any action from the account holder.

Avalanche Method: A type of debt repayment strategy that focuses on paying down debt with the highest amount of interest first.

Balance: The amount of money in your bank account.

Budget: A finance plan that allocates future personal income towards expenses, savings, debt repayment, and investing.

Certificates of Deposits: A type of savings account that earns interest over a certain time frame.

Certified Financial Planner: A financial professional that can advise clients on financial topics such as retirement, investments, tax planning, goal setting, and risk management.

Certified Financial Therapist: A certified professional who provides therapy services with the goal of changing the way you think, feel, and behave about money.

Checking Account: A type of bank account that allows for deposits and withdrawals.

Collateral: An asset pledged to secure a loan.

Community Property: Assets or debts acquired during marriage.

Credit Card: A card issued by a financial services company or bank that allows cardholders to borrow money.

Credit Report: A detailed record of an individual's credit history over time.

Credit Score: A number that represents an individual's creditworthiness.

Credit Union: A non-for-profit financial institution owned and controlled by its members.

Debit Card: A card issued by a bank or financial institution that is linked to a checking or savings account.

Debt: the amount of money owed to the lender by the borrower.

Debt Collection: The process of pursuing agreed-upon debt payments.

Debt Collector: An individual or agency that regularly collects debts owed to others.

Debt Consolidation: A debt management strategy that combines multiple debts into a single loan with a single monthly payment.

Direct Deposit: The way to electronically deposit money into a checking and/or savings account.

Emergency Fund: A separate savings account or cash reserve used for unexpected expenses.

Expenses - Fixed: Expenses that remain the same each month.

Expenses - Periodic: Expenses that do not occur monthly, but happen sporadically throughout the year.

Expenses - Variable: Expenses that may change from month-to-month.

Family Justice Center: A center where victims of domestic violence, assault, abuse, and human trafficking can receive financial, legal, and housing services in their community.

Financial Abuse: A form of abuse that gives one partner control and power in a relationship, leaving the other partner trapped.

Financial Infidelity: A form of abuse in which one partner intentionally lies about money to the other.

High Yield Savings Account: A type of savings account that pays higher interest rate compared to a traditional savings account.

Income: Money received in exchange for your labor or through investments.

Income - Fixed: Money that is set at a particular amount and does not vary.

Income - Variable: Money that is not set at a particular amount and changes over time.

Installment Debt: A lump sum of money given to you upfront and is repaid through regular, fixed payments over a set period of time.

Interest: The cost of borrowing money or the return earned on savings and investments.

Liability: Something that a person, company, or organization owes, usually in the form of money.

Loan: Something that is borrowed and expected to be paid back with interest.

Maintenance Fee: A charge you pay monthly for having a checking and/or savings account with a bank.

Revolving Debt: An ongoing line of credit that you can borrow from as needed.

Secured Debt: A type of debt that requires collateral, which the lender has a lien on.

Self-help Legal Center: A center that provides free legal resources and information to people who are representing themselves in court without a lawyer.

Separate Property: Assets or debts acquired before marriage.

Snowball Method: A type of debt repayment strategy that focuses on paying down debt with the lowest amount first.

Traditional Savings Account: A type of savings account offered by banks and credit unions.

Unsecured Debt: A type of debt that does not require collateral.

Resources

National Resources

Alliance for HOPE International
www.allianceforhope.com

American Immigration Lawyers Association
www.aila.org

Battered Women's Justice Project
www.bwj.org

Battered Women's Legal Advocacy Project
www.bylap.org

Domestic Abuse Intervention Project
www.duluth-model.org

Futures Without Violence
www.futureswithoutviolence.org

National Coalition Against Domestic Violence
www.ncadv.org

National Criminal Justice Reference Service
www.ncjrs.org

National Domestic Violence Hotline
www.thehotline.org

National Immigration Project of the National Lawyers Guild
www.national-immigrationproject.org

National Institute of Justice
www.ojp.usdoj.gov/nij

RAINN (Rape, Abuse & Incesent National Network)
www.rainn.org

WomensLaw
www.womenslaw.org

Housing and Shelter

Domestic Shelters
www.domesticshelters.org

Safe Horizon
www.safehorizon.org

Legal Resources

Legal Aid Society
www.legalaid.org

VictimConnect
www.victimconnect.org

Family Justice Center Alliance
www.familyjusticecenter.org

Financial Resources

Annual Credit Report
www.annualcreditreport.com

Credit Karma
www.creditkarma.com

Equifax
www.equifax.com

Experian
www.experian.com

Transunion
www.transunion.com

National Foundation for Credit Counseling
www.nfcc.org

Financial Counseling Association of America
www.fcaa.org

For more resources, go to www.justinedeperalta.com

About the Author

Justine **De Peralta** is a former classroom teacher turned Certified Financial Educator (CFEI®), Money Coach, and Domestic Violence Counselor. As the founder of Afraid to Affluent, she specializes in helping BIPOC women and domestic violence survivors develop the  confidence and financial literacy skills needed to navigate challenging financial situations.

Her commitment to supporting BIPOC women and domestic violence survivors began in 2007. For three years, she served at a local courthouse, helping individuals dealing with divorce, child custody, and eviction. Although there are many reasons couples seek divorce, financial challenges and domestic violence are among the most common.

Despite building a career in education, Justine transitioned to financial services after leaving a physically, emotionally, and psychologically abusive marriage. Her dedication to helping those in abusive and toxic relationships is deeply personal and fuels her passion for this work.

She knows firsthand the struggles of navigating difficult financial situations: having no emergency fund, accumulating high credit card debt, living paycheck to paycheck, going into collections, and hitting financial rock bottom.

But guess what? She also knows how to bounce back STRONGER, SMARTER, HEALTHIER, and WEALTHIER. Now, Justine is passionate about teaching women and domestic violence survivors how to reclaim their confidence and become money smart, body strong!

www.justinedeperalta.com
Instagram: @msfinancialfit
Twitter: @msfinancialfit

Work With Me

If you're ready to take the next step, I offer a range of services to help you at every phase of your financial journey.

1-ON-1 COACHING

After reading this book, you now have the knowledge and skills needed to build a financial safety net. If you're looking to receive personalized guidance tailored specifically to your financial needs, I offer 1-on-1 coaching to help you achieve your financial goals.

These sessions are all about you! We will work together to create a customized financial plan with clear, actionable steps to move you closer to financial independence.

GROUP COACHING

Looking for like-minded individuals on the same path towards financial healing and independence? My group coaching sessions offer a collaborative and supportive environment where we tackle a variety of financial topics together.

These sessions take place over several weeks with the same group, allowing you to learn from each other's experiences and to make lasting connections.

FINANCIAL WORKSHOPS

These are not your typical sit-and-get workshops. My workshops are personalized and designed to provide a hands-on learning experience. By the end of each workshop, participants are equipped with the tools and knowledge needed to make intentional money decisions.

Depending on the needs of the audience, each workshop is different. These interactive sessions are great for organizations, schools, or community groups looking to gain the confidence and knowledge needed to level up their finances!

SPEAKING EVENTS

Are you looking for an engaging speaker for your next event? I offer personalized presentations on a variety of financial topics that fit the needs of your audience. Whether it's a conference, seminar, or event, I deliver practical insights and strategies that inspire and empower participants to take positive action in their daily lives.

To learn more about my services and how I might be able to help you, book a free Discovery Call with me by visiting www.justinedeperalta.com to learn more!

> "Before meeting with Justine I was lost, scared, and a little embarrassed about my finances. I knew I had debt (student

loans, dental, credit card) but I was overwhelmed and didn't know where to start. I landed a new better paying job and didn't know how to manage my money. Since working with her, I have less worry and stress about finances. My relationship with money has improved and I'm more confident and financially literate. It was nice to have a non-judgmental & unbiased person to sort my finances with. I have more control over my money, I'm paying off debt, and most importantly I have a plan! I never would have gotten here without Justine and her uplifting and empowering demeanor. Thank you Justine!"

— *Elizabeth B., Therapist*

Thank you so much for reading my book!

I hope you found tremendous value in this book and feel empowered to take action towards a better and fulfilling life.

Your thoughts and feedback are incredibly valuable to me and the future readers of this book.

If you found this book insightful, invaluable, or inspiring, please take a few minutes to leave an honest and helpful review. Your review doesn't need to be long— just a few sentences can make a big difference!

You can share your thoughts by leaving a review at www.justinedeperalta.com/review

or

by scanning the QR code below:

Thank you so much for your support. I'm grateful we can be on this journey together!

Big hug,

Justine